D1428984

BIBLE
LANDS

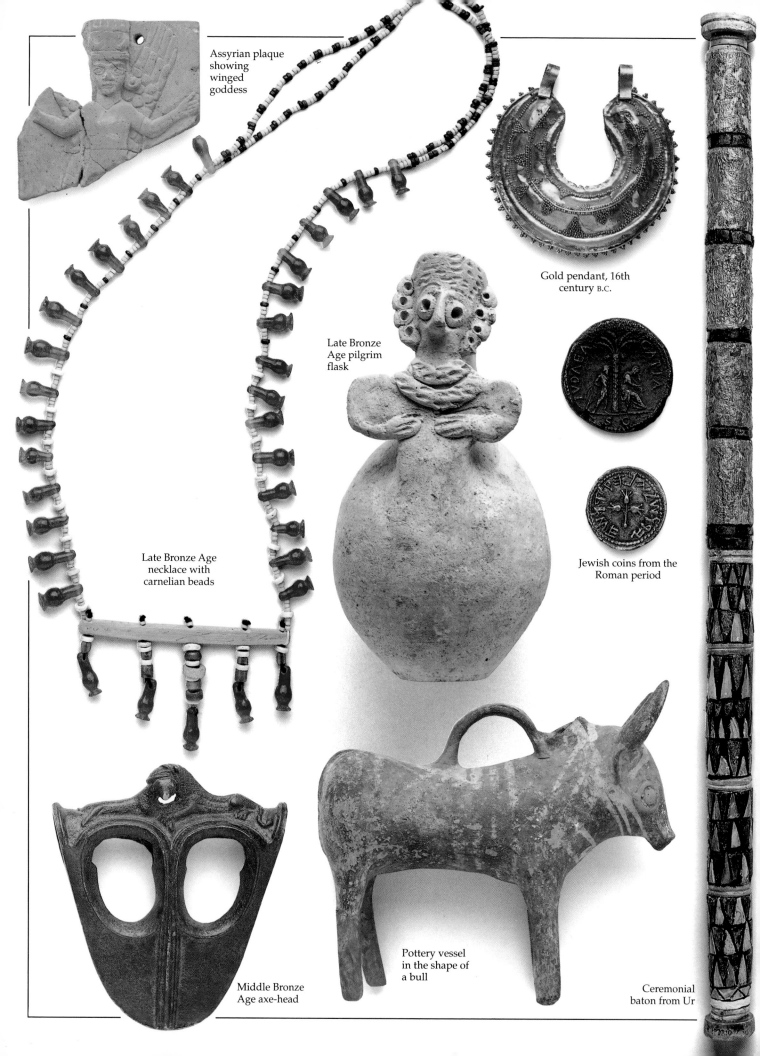

Assyrian plaque showing winged goddess

Gold pendant, 16th century B.C.

Late Bronze Age pilgrim flask

Late Bronze Age necklace with carnelian beads

Jewish coins from the Roman period

Middle Bronze Age axe-head

Pottery vessel in the shape of a bull

Ceremonial baton from Ur

Gold earrings from
the Roman period

Bronze
and gold
toggle pins

EYEWITNESS GUIDES

BIBLE LANDS

Written by

JONATHAN N. TUBB

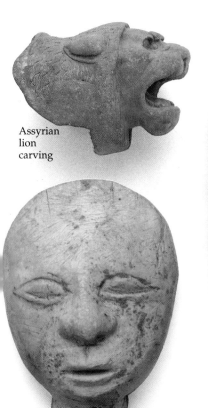

Assyrian
lion
carving

Ivory plaque
from Nimrud,
8th century B.C.

Ivory carved
head, 13th
century B.C.

Phoenician
glass
vessels

DK

DORLING KINDERSLEY
London • New York • Stuttgart
in association with
THE BRITISH MUSEUM • LONDON

Ivory duck's head
found at Lachish

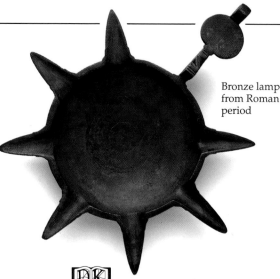

Bronze lamp
from Roman
period

Frieze showing Persian palace guard

Persian
silver bowl

Selection of
arrowheads

Egyptian-style seal

Carved ivory found at Nimrud

Persian
silver stag

DK

A DORLING KINDERSLEY BOOK

Project editor Phil Wilkinson
Art editor Martin Atcherley
Senior editor Helen Parker
Senior art editor Julia Harris
Production Louise Barratt
Picture research Diana Morris
Special photography Alan Hills and Barbara Winter
of the British Museum, Karl Shone

This Eyewitness ® Guide has been conceived by Dorling
Kindersley Limited and Editions Gallimard

First published in Great Britain in 1991 by Dorling Kindersley
Limited, 9 Henrietta Street, London WC2E 8PS

Reprinted 1994, 1995

Copyright © 1991 Dorling Kindersley Limited, London

A CIP catalogue record for this book is available from the
British Library

ISBN 0 86318 625 4

Colour reproduction by Colourscan, Singapore
Printed in Singapore by Toppan

Contents

Ivory carving showing winged sphinx

Lands of the Bible

THE HOLY LAND is a region of great diversity. From west to east four different kinds of terrain are found. The coastal plain is low-lying and dry in the south, narrowing to the north with stretches of marsh and lagoon. The second zone is the hill country behind the coast, well watered and fertile on the west-facing slopes and rising to rocky ridges that form the spine of the hill country. The third zone, the Jordan Valley, is almost rainless. The highlands of Jordan and the plateau beyond make up the fourth zone. There are rugged mountains in the south of the highlands and rolling hills to the north. The plateau is made up of farmland, giving way to dry steppe country (treeless plains) and finally desert.

Landscape near the Dead Sea

By the Dead Sea, looking east to the hills of Moab

Village of Dir-Zamet, near Hebron

MOUNT HERMON

LAKE HULEH

Dan

Hazor

Capernaum

SEA OF GALILEE

Tiberias

GILEAD

JORDAN RIVER

Tell es-Sa'idiyeh

Tiwal esh-Sharqi

Beth shan

UPPER GALILEE

LOWER GALILEE

Tirzah

PLAIN OF PHOENICIA

Nazareth

Tyre

Megiddo

Samaria

Acre

Caesarea

MEDITERRANEAN SEA

"Lot's wife" – a pillar of rock near the Dead Sea

THE BIBLE LANDS
The Holy Land, also referred to at different times in its history as Palestine and Canaan, lies in the Levant (the eastern Mediterranean). This map shows some of the most important places mentioned in this book, together with the seas and lakes and the River Jordan. North is to the left-hand side of the map.

View of Jerusalem by Carl Werner (1809-94)

Mount Sinai, south of the map area, was the scene of many of the Old Testament stories

Landscape by the Sea of Galilee

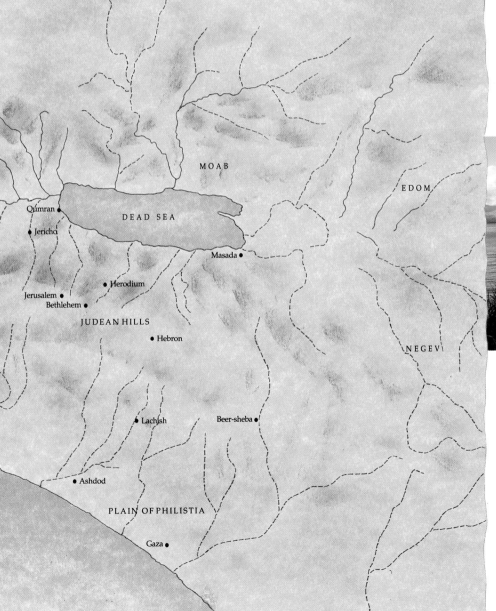

Modern fishing boats on the Sea of Galilee

CHRONOLOGY OF THE BIBLE LANDS	
Paleolithic (Old Stone Age)	700,000-15,000 B.C.
Mesolithic (Middle Stone Age)	15,000-8,300 B.C.
Neolithic (New Stone Age)	8,300-4,500 B.C.
Chalcolithic	4500-3200 B.C.
Early Bronze Age	3200-2000 B.C.
Middle Bronze Age	2000-1550 B.C.
Late Bronze Age	1550-1150 B.C.
Iron Age	1200-586 B.C.
Babylonian and Persian Periods	586-332 B.C.
Hellenistic Period	332-37 B.C.
Roman Period	37 B.C.-A.D. 324
Byzantine Period	A.D. 324-640
Early Arab Period	A.D. 640-1099

Early ancestors

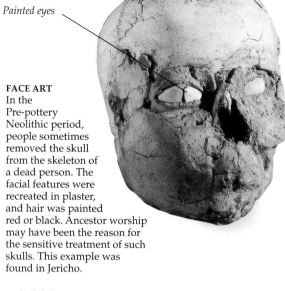

Painted eyes

FACE ART
In the Pre-pottery Neolithic period, people sometimes removed the skull from the skeleton of a dead person. The facial features were recreated in plaster, and hair was painted red or black. Ancestor worship may have been the reason for the sensitive treatment of such skulls. This example was found in Jericho.

MUCH OF OUR KNOWLEDGE of the early prehistory of the Holy Land comes from the site of Jericho, near the northern end of the Red Sea. Here, excavations have uncovered a remarkable series of settlements dating back to about 10,000 B.C., when Middle Stone Age (Mesolithic) hunters settled there permanently. At first they built flimsy shelters of sticks and hides, but these were later replaced by proper houses built of sun-dried mud bricks. In settling down, these people took the all-important step which led in the end to cultivating domestic crops and domesticating animals – a process known as the "Neolithic revolution". Jericho was not alone. During the following 3,000 years small farming villages sprang up all over the area. During the New Stone Age (or Neolithic, about 8000-4500 B.C.) stone, flint, and obsidian (a type of volcanic glass) were used for tools and weapons. The early, pre-pottery phase of the Neolithic is remarkable for its arts and crafts – weaving, basketry, carpentry, and sculpture. Pottery was first made in around 5500 B.C. Knowledge of copper smelting was acquired about 1,000 years later, during the period known as the Chalcolithic (from the Greek word for copper).

FIRST CITY
In the Pre-pottery Neolithic period Jericho grew in a remarkable way. In contrast to the usual simple, unwalled villages, it became a real city, with massive walls and at least one large stone tower, seen here.

SCRAPER
Even after copper-working began, flint implements continued to be used. One type is the "fan scraper", which might have been used for preparing animal skins for clothing.

STONY FACE
This finely carved limestone face mask dates to the Pre-pottery Neolithic period. It comes from er-Ram, near Jerusalem.

Fan scraper

Scraper

8

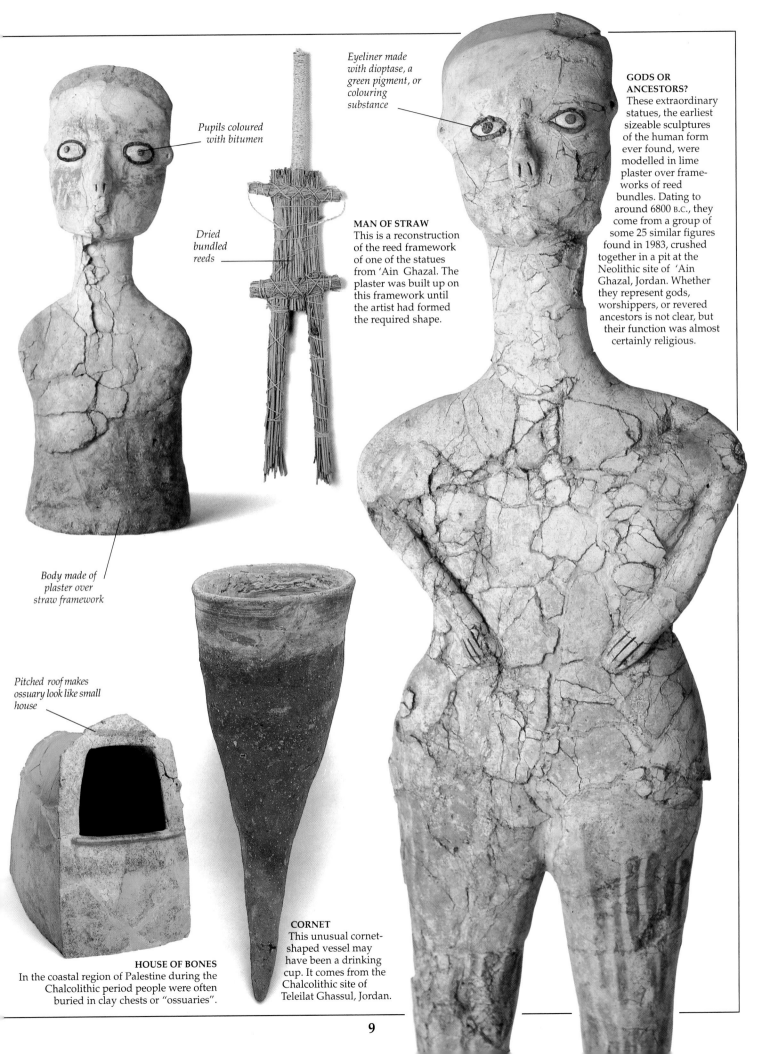

Pupils coloured
with bitumen

*Eyeliner made
with dioptase, a
green pigment, or
colouring
substance*

MAN OF STRAW
This is a reconstruction
of the reed framework
of one of the statues
from 'Ain Ghazal. The
plaster was built up on
this framework until
the artist had formed
the required shape.

*Dried
bundled
reeds*

**GODS OR
ANCESTORS?**
These extraordinary
statues, the earliest
sizeable sculptures
of the human form
ever found, were
modelled in lime
plaster over frame-
works of reed
bundles. Dating to
around 6800 B.C., they
come from a group of
some 25 similar figures
found in 1983, crushed
together in a pit at the
Neolithic site of 'Ain
Ghazal, Jordan. Whether
they represent gods,
worshippers, or revered
ancestors is not clear, but
their function was almost
certainly religious.

*Body made of
plaster over
straw framework*

*Pitched roof makes
ossuary look like small
house*

HOUSE OF BONES
In the coastal region of Palestine during the
Chalcolithic period people were often
buried in clay chests or "ossuaries".

CORNET
This unusual cornet-
shaped vessel may
have been a drinking
cup. It comes from the
Chalcolithic site of
Teleilat Ghassul, Jordan.

9

The patriarchs

ABRAHAM, ISAAC, JACOB, AND JOSEPH were the patriarchs of the book of Genesis. They are seen as the "founding fathers" of what was to become Israel. Archaeology has provided a wealth of information about the time in which their stories are set, and the cultures of the lands through which they are believed to have travelled. The patriarchal stories may have happened between about 2600 and 1800 B.C., with the tales of Abraham being the earliest, those of Joseph in Egypt the latest. Traditionally, Abraham is said to have gone from Ur in Iraq to Canaan, by way of Harran in Turkey. Although there is no archaeological proof that this journey took place, there is little doubt that it could have been made.

A gold shell used as a cosmetic container, used in Ur about 4,000 years ago

PATRIARCHS' PATH
This map shows the areas between which the patriarchs travelled. They could have gone with trading caravans, or followed the Bedouin, learning the skills of nomadic life.

ROYAL RICHES
At the time of Abraham's departure, Ur was a prosperous city. Many of the graves excavated by Sir Leonard Woolley in the 1920s and 1930s were found to contain expensive gifts for the afterlife, such as this ceremonial baton ornamented with gold, lapis lazuli, and mother-of-pearl.

GOLDEN GLORY
An idea of the wealth of the royal family of Ur can be gained from the objects found in their graves, such as this fine gold chalice.

TEMPLE TOWER
One of the most important buildings at Ur was the ziggurat, a type of tower, built of mud bricks, several storeys high, with a temple on top. The biblical Tower of Babel (in the city of Babylon) would have been a similar structure.

Simple bow

Lyre – remains of similar instruments found at Ur

Tunic made of coloured and embroidered wool

Bellows, suggesting that some of the visitors were metalworkers

Duck-bill axe (p. 47)

Donkey, one of the earliest beasts of burden

Women wear shoes, in contrast to the men's sandals

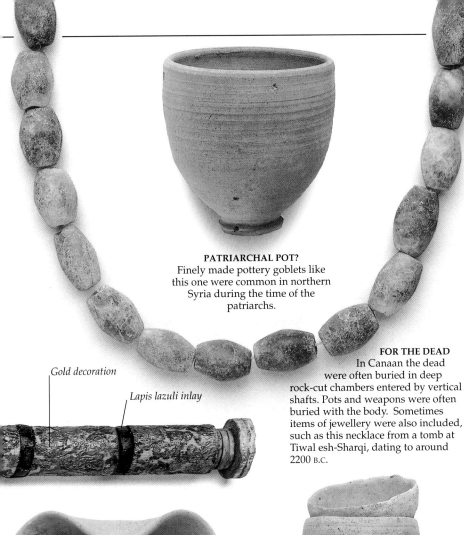

PATRIARCHAL POT?
Finely made pottery goblets like this one were common in northern Syria during the time of the patriarchs.

Gold decoration

Lapis lazuli inlay

FOR THE DEAD
In Canaan the dead were often buried in deep rock-cut chambers entered by vertical shafts. Pots and weapons were often buried with the body. Sometimes items of jewellery were also included, such as this necklace from a tomb at Tiwal esh-Sharqi, dating to around 2200 B.C.

DRINKER'S DELIGHT
This unusual flask from North Syria was a device for raising liquid. Fluid entered through holes in the base, and could be retained by clamping a thumb over the narrow mouth. The liquid could then be released by removing the thumb pressure.

FISHY FLAME
In the patriarchal period the people of Canaan used fish oil in their lamps. It gave such low light that four wicks were needed.

YOGHURT-MAKER
Yoghurt (known as leben) has always been an important food in the Levant. This pair of vessels from Jordan is thought to have been used for making yoghurt.

Sickle sword

Woollen kilt

Group's leader is called Absha

VISITORS FROM CANAAN
The stories of Joseph's adventures in Egypt are best set in the period 2000-1800 B.C., when archaeological evidence has shown that Asiatic people were entering Egypt. These wall-paintings are from the tomb of an Egyptian called Amenemhet at Beni Hasan. They show a group of Asiatics, probably Canaanites, being introduced to the Egyptian court.

Egypt

IN THE EARLY BRONZE AGE the opening of trade routes to Egypt allowed a thriving city-based economy to develop in Canaan. In the Middle Bronze Age, groups of Canaanites moved into the Egyptian Delta and established a local dynasty called the Hyksos, who eventually took over the whole of Egypt. Only in the Late Bronze Age, around 1550 B.C., did the Egyptian pharaohs expel the Hyksos, launch a military campaign against Canaan, and bring it under Egyptian control. Egypt imposed heavy taxes on Canaan, but in return the Canaanite cities gained security and better access to international markets. In the reign of Ramesses II (1304-1287 B.C.), the empire was reorganized. Key strategic cities like Beth Shan and Gaza were strengthened, others were allowed to decline. Many people were made homeless and migrated to the Judean hill country where they established small farming settlements. These dispossessed Canaanites, known to the Egyptians as Hapiru (or Hebrews), formed the basis of what was to become Israel.

LOST AND FOUND
According to the Bible, Moses, leader of the Hebrew exodus, was found in the bullrushes.

POWER SYMBOL
This Egyptian ceremonial axe has an elaborate openwork head.

EGYPT AND CANAAN
In the Late Bronze Age Canaan became part of the Egyptian empire. Her local rulers became vassals of the pharaoh. Some of the cities of Canaan, like Gaza, proospered under the Egyptians.

LETTER TO THE PHARAOH
The Armana letters contain reports from vassal rulers of the empire to Egyptian pharaoh Amenophis III. Some mention trouble caused by lawless bands of "Hapiru", homeless peoples living on the fringes of cities. The Hapiru are related to the biblical Hebrews.

STRONGHOLD
Beth Shan was one of the major centres of Egyptian control in Canaan. During the time of Ramesses II, the city was strongly garrisoned and had an Egyptian governor.

HEBREW SLAVES?
Both the Bible and an Egyptian papyrus refer to Hapiru employed as labourers in Ramesses II's building projects. They may not actually have been slaves, as suggested in this detail of a painting by 19th-century artist Sir Edward Poynter.

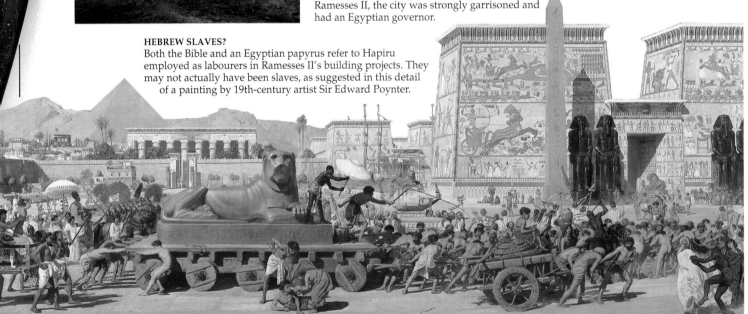

The Philistines

In Ramesses III's reign (1198-1166 B.C.), the Egyptian empire faced a major crisis when it was invaded by a league of peoples from the Aegean or southern Anatolia. Known as the Sea Peoples, they included a group called the Philistines. Ramesses pushed them back from the shores of Egpyt in a great naval battle. But he could not stop them settling in Canaan, at the southern end of the coastal strip.

PHILISTINE FACE
The Philistines, like some of the other Sea Peoples, buried their dead in distinctive "slipper-shaped" coffins. The lids show rather grotesquely modelled human features.

FINE FEATHERS
Philistine warriors wore feathered headdresses.

SUCCESSFUL PHARAOH
Ramesses II brought to an end Egypt's long conflict with the Hittites of Anatolia. After fighting the Hittites at the Battle of Qadesh in 1289 B.C., the Egyptians signed a peace treaty which brought them a period of peace and prosperity. Ramesses II was most probably the pharaoh of the biblical exodus.

Striped headcloth indicates kingship

After Ramesses II reorganized his empire the number of hill-farming settlements in Judea increased dramatically.

PARTING OF THE WATERS
Although archaeology cannot confirm the story of the Hebrew exodus through the waters of the Red Sea, it is not unlikely that a group of Hapiru left Egypt during the reign of Ramesses II and found their way to the Judean hill country.

Living on a mound

T HE PEOPLE OF the Middle and Late Bronze Ages in Palestine are traditionally known as the Canaanites. But the distinctive Canaanite culture did not appear fully formed at the beginning of this period: it developed gradually and its origins can be traced back to the 4th millennium B.C. By this time, the people of Egypt, Syria, and Mesopotamia had formed cities and developed systems of writing. The growth of trade routes led to similar developments in Palestine. Many of the small villages of the Chalcolithic period were abandoned. New groups of people entering the country around 3200 B.C. established themselves at new sites chosen for their natural resources, and designed to benefit from the growing web of trade connections. Often, these sites would be settled for thousands of years afterwards. As generation after generation lived and built upon the same spot, huge artificial mounds of debris (household rubbish and the foundations of old houses) built up. These mounds, still visible today, are known as tells.

Portrait of a Canaanite, a Late Bronze Age ivory from Lachish

Canaanite pottery of the Early Bronze Age, like this jug, is elegant and well made.

A "section", a vertical cross-section through the tell, revealing walls, floors, layers of ash and rubbish, pits, ovens, and other features that show the site's history of occupation

The Citadel that dominates present-day Aleppo in Syria is an example of a tell that has been occupied continuously until quite recently

WHAT DOES IT TELL US?
A tell provides the archaeologist with invaluable information about the past. Much of it consists of layers of accumulated mud bricks, the standard building material of the Holy Land. This material represents the phases of habitation of the site, and through careful excavation, can show the archaeologist the history of the site's occupation in reverse order. This model tell is based on Tell Deir 'Alla, Jordan, the biblical city of Succoth. The model shows the various methods of archaeology used at different sites to disentangle the complicated sequences of occupational phases.

THE CITY OF LACHISH
This reconstruction of Lachish shows the tell as it might have been at the time of the siege in 701 B.C. (p. 46). The two walls are clearly visible, as is the strongly fortified gateway.

MOUNTING DEFENCES
By the time of the Middle Bronze Age many of the major tell sites had risen to considerable heights, and were becoming rather unstable around the edges. So the inhabitants strengthened the sides and added a coat of plaster to them. This created a smooth slope called a "glacis", which provided a good defensive barrier. At the top of the glacis a tall defensive rampart was made and this was crowned by the city wall itself. The base of the glacis was held in by a strong retaining wall and a ditch (or "fosse") around the base of the mound completed the defences. Elaborate gateways, like the one at Tell Dan, northern Israel, were built into the walls.

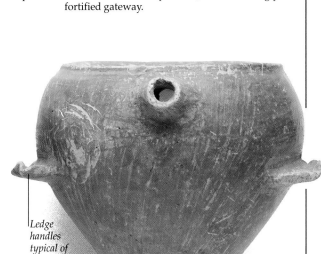

EXPENSIVE TASTES
The Canaanites liked to have attractive things around them. This jar is made of faience. It was found at Lachish and imported from Egypt.

Ledge handles typical of Canaanite pottery of this period

POURER
The highly burnished finish of this pot is called "red slip". This was a popular surface treatment for Early Bronze Age table wares. The vessel has a spout for pouring and typical ledge handles.

Mud-brick buildings, often difficult to distinguish from surrounding soil

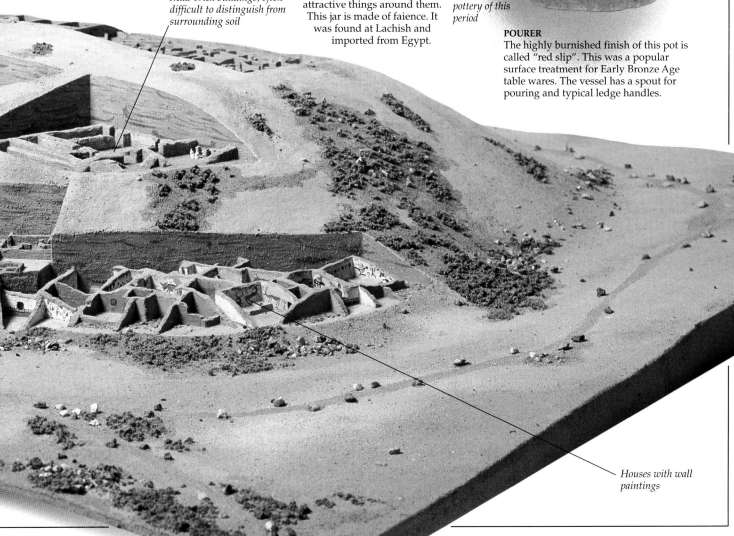

Houses with wall paintings

The Canaanites

THE FULL FLOWERING of Canaanite culture came in the Middle Bronze Age (c. 2000-1550 B.C.). During this period Canaan was largely free of the power struggles and foreign interventions that were to dominate its later history. In this climate, the country developed an ever-expanding trade network. There was extensive trade with Egypt, and contacts were strengthened with Syria, Anatolia, and Cyprus. Canaan's art, architecture, and craftsmanship reached new levels of skill and sophistication as her artists were influenced by a variety of sources and countries, blending them to make their own style. During the Late Bronze Age (1550-1150 B.C.) Canaan was dominated by Egypt. The Egyptian empire brought with it even more far-reaching trade links, including those with the Mycenaean people of mainland Greece. But the local culture, by now well established, continued to flourish.

THE LAND OF CANAAN
We do not know exactly how Palestine was structured politically during the Middle Bronze Age. It was probably made up of a large number of independent city states, each ruled by a prince. Each city would have controlled its own area of land containing a number of dependent towns and villages.

STAR ATTRACTION
This finely made star pendant from Tell el-'Ajjul shows the skill of the Canaanite goldsmiths of the 16th century B.C.

POTS AND PALMS
Canaanite pots of the Late Bronze Age are ofen decorated with this motif of palm trees and ibexes. The palm tree on this goblet from Lachish is highly stylized.

SMALL DIPPER
"Dippers" were little jugs used to take liquid out of a larger container. People would often push a stick through the handle of the dipper and hang it over the mouth of a store jar.

PILGRIM'S PLEASURE
The Canaanites were very inventive. This amusing pilgrim flask, dating to the end of the Late Bronze Age, has its own built-in drinking cup.

COALS TO NEWCASTLE
Egyptian-style seals and scarabs (seals in the shape of a beetle), were used to denote ownership, and were common in Canaan. Many were made by Canaanite craftsmen, and some were even imported to Egypt.

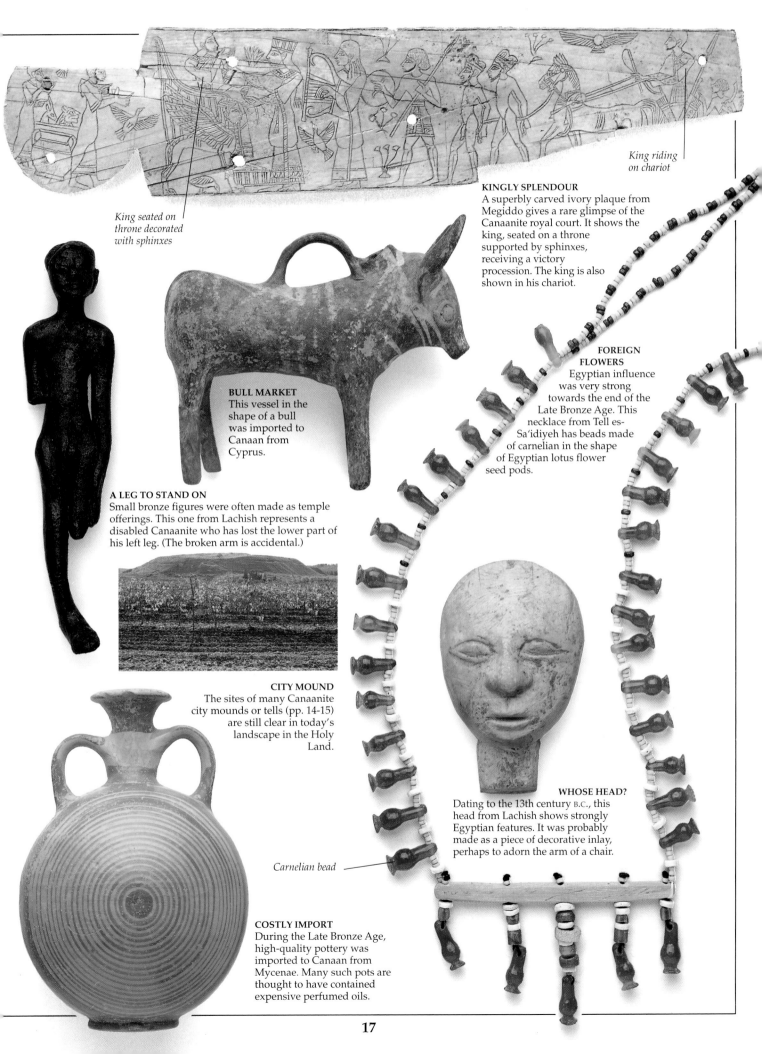

*King seated on
throne decorated
with sphinxes*

*King riding
on chariot*

KINGLY SPLENDOUR
A superbly carved ivory plaque from
Megiddo gives a rare glimpse of the
Canaanite royal court. It shows the
king, seated on a throne
supported by sphinxes,
receiving a victory
procession. The king is also
shown in his chariot.

BULL MARKET
This vessel in the
shape of a bull
was imported to
Canaan from
Cyprus.

**FOREIGN
FLOWERS**
Egyptian influence
was very strong
towards the end of the
Late Bronze Age. This
necklace from Tell es-
Sa'idiyeh has beads made
of carnelian in the shape
of Egyptian lotus flower
seed pods.

A LEG TO STAND ON
Small bronze figures were often made as temple
offerings. This one from Lachish represents a
disabled Canaanite who has lost the lower part of
his left leg. (The broken arm is accidental.)

CITY MOUND
The sites of many Canaanite
city mounds or tells (pp. 14-15)
are still clear in today's
landscape in the Holy
Land.

WHOSE HEAD?
Dating to the 13th century B.C., this
head from Lachish shows strongly
Egyptian features. It was probably
made as a piece of decorative inlay,
perhaps to adorn the arm of a chair.

Carnelian bead

COSTLY IMPORT
During the Late Bronze Age,
high-quality pottery was
imported to Canaan from
Mycenae. Many such pots are
thought to have contained
expensive perfumed oils.

Death and burial

ANCIENT PEOPLE always made efforts to treat their dead with great care. In the Holy Land this often involved producing elaborate graves, sometimes dug deeply into the natural rock. Burial, rather than cremation, was the usual practice, and a belief in the afterlife is shown from the earliest periods – not only from the religious writings of historical times but also from the evidence of the graves themselves. From the earliest times the deceased was accompanied with grave goods (items needed for the afterlife), such as jewellery, pottery, tools, and weapons. Food and drink were also included. Excavating such burials gives the archaeologist a rich source of information about the people themselves – their beliefs, the objects they used and cherished, their physical characteristics, and even the diseases that afflicted them. The objects shown here come from a child's grave, excavated at Tell es-Sa'idiyeh, Jordan, the biblical city of Zarethan.

FASTENER
This pin, found near the left shoulder of the skeleton, would have fastened the shroud in which the child was buried.

BRIGHT BRACELET
The girl wore a bracelet of carnelian and silver beads on her left wrist.

A silver finger ring was worn on the left hand

LUCKY CHARM?
A simple ring carved out of steatite (soapstone) was found, not on the girl's finger, but on top of her chest. It may originally have been held on a string around her neck.

ONE BY ONE
Earrings, like this silver one, were often worn singly. This one, found beneath the skull, was probably worn on the left ear.

FINE DECORATION
Bronze bangles were worn as jewellery throughout the Iron Age. This pair have delicate incised decoration. They were worn as anklets.

ON THE HEAD
This unusual clasp was found placed on top of the skull. It may have been fixed to a cap, perhaps to attach a tassel.

Incised decoration on terminal (end) of bangle

Grooves to hold thread

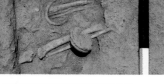

THE ANKLETS IN POSITION
This detail of the girl's lower legs show the bronze anklets in the position in which they were found.

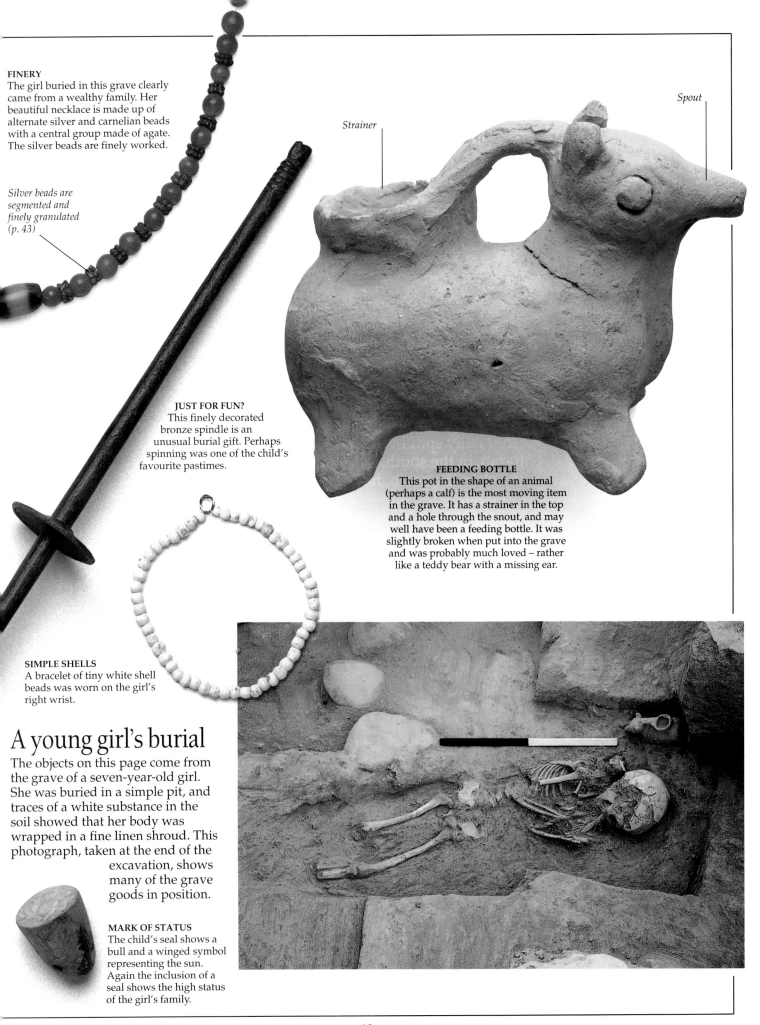

FINERY
The girl buried in this grave clearly came from a wealthy family. Her beautiful necklace is made up of alternate silver and carnelian beads with a central group made of agate. The silver beads are finely worked.

Silver beads are segmented and finely granulated (p. 43)

JUST FOR FUN?
This finely decorated bronze spindle is an unusual burial gift. Perhaps spinning was one of the child's favourite pastimes.

Strainer

Spout

FEEDING BOTTLE
This pot in the shape of an animal (perhaps a calf) is the most moving item in the grave. It has a strainer in the top and a hole through the snout, and may well have been a feeding bottle. It was slightly broken when put into the grave and was probably much loved – rather like a teddy bear with a missing ear.

SIMPLE SHELLS
A bracelet of tiny white shell beads was worn on the girl's right wrist.

A young girl's burial

The objects on this page come from the grave of a seven-year-old girl. She was buried in a simple pit, and traces of a white substance in the soil showed that her body was wrapped in a fine linen shroud. This photograph, taken at the end of the excavation, shows many of the grave goods in position.

MARK OF STATUS
The child's seal shows a bull and a winged symbol representing the sun. Again the inclusion of a seal shows the high status of the girl's family.

19

Delicate ivory
furniture ornament
from Samaria

The Israelites

By ABOUT 1150 B.C., the Egpytians had effectively withdrawn from Canaan, leaving a vacuum to be filled by the Israelites and the Philistines. For nearly 100 years they lived side by side, the Philistines on the coastal plain, the Israelites in the more barren hill country. But during the 11th century B.C., the Philistines tried to extend their territory. Faced with this threat, the Israelites united into one nation, under the leadership of first Saul then David. In about 1000 B.C. David captured Jerusalem and was proclaimed king of the Israelite nation. He finally defeated the Philistines and expanded Israel's territory. The kingdom continued to flourish under David's son Solomon, who extended Israel's trading network and built the great Temple in Jerusalem. After Solomon's death in 928 B.C., tensions between the north and south of the kingdom came to a head. The monarchy finally split in two. The capital of Judah, in the south, was Jerusalem; Israel, in the north, had its capital at Samaria.

NO SMOKE WITHOUT FIRE
This lively 19th-century engraving represents the destruction of the Temple by the Babylonians in 587 B.C.

Porch

Bronze columns called Jachin and Boaz

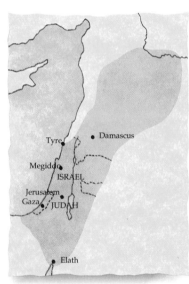

THE TWO KINGDOMS
This map shows the area of David's kingdom, which divided into two: Israel in the north and Judah in the south.

FIRST MENTION OF ISRAEL
This stela of the pharaoh Merneptah (1235-1223 B.C.) records a military campaign in Canaan directed against Gezer, Ashkelon, and Israel. This is the first recorded mention of Israel as a political unit, representing the farming communities of the Judean hill country.

BOTTOMS UP
Probably a furniture ornament, this ivory fragment from King Ahab's palace at Samaria shows the hindquarters of a lion. Relations between Israel and Phoenicia were close, and Phoenician artisans were often used for fine work such as this.

Solomon's temple

Wealth from trade, and a good central administration, enabled Solomon to carry out large-scale building projects. Impressive public buildings, gateways, and city walls were built at several major sites. The most important project was the Temple in Jerusalem. No traces of the building can be seen now, but there are detailed descriptions of it in the Bible. This evidence, together with excavations of other sites, have made possible various reconstructions of the Temple like the one shown here.

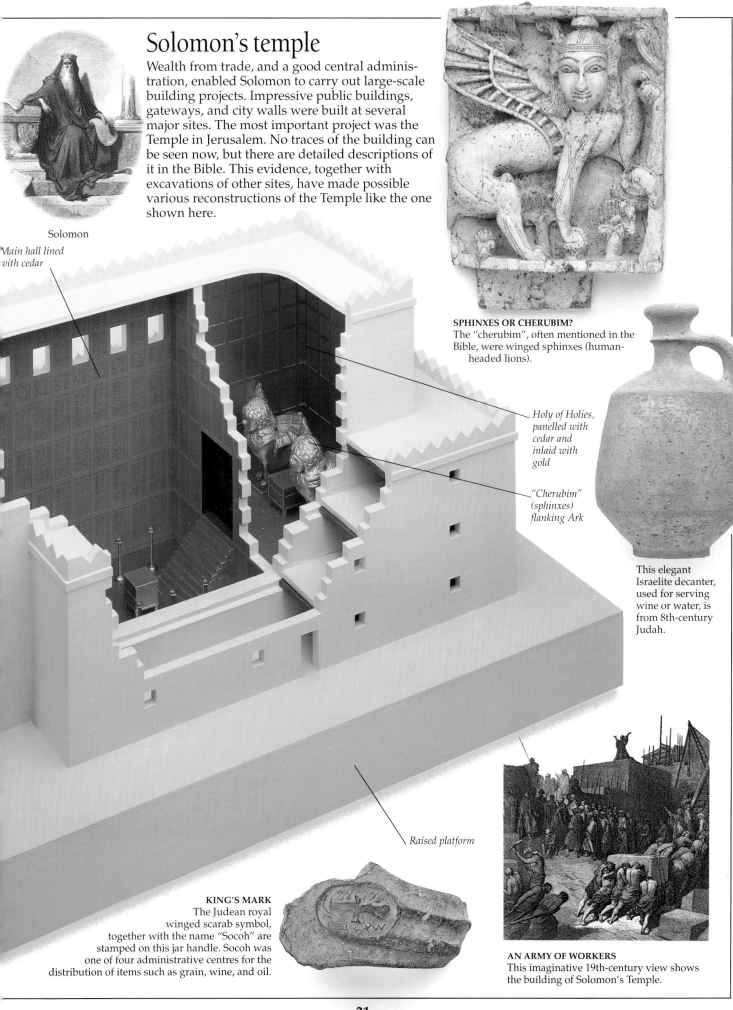

Solomon

Main hall lined with cedar

SPHINXES OR CHERUBIM?
The "cherubim", often mentioned in the Bible, were winged sphinxes (human-headed lions).

Holy of Holies, panelled with cedar and inlaid with gold

"Cherubim" (sphinxes) flanking Ark

This elegant Israelite decanter, used for serving wine or water, is from 8th-century Judah.

Raised platform

KING'S MARK
The Judean royal winged scarab symbol, together with the name "Socoh" are stamped on this jar handle. Socoh was one of four administrative centres for the distribution of items such as grain, wine, and oil.

AN ARMY OF WORKERS
This imaginative 19th-century view shows the building of Solomon's Temple.

21

The Phoenicians

The Phoenician writing on this seal identifies its owner as "Tamak-el, son of Milkam"

Bᴦ ᴛʜᴇ ꜱᴇᴄᴏɴᴅ ᴍɪʟʟᴇɴɴɪᴜᴍ ʙ.ᴄ. the Israelites occupied most of Palestine except for the southern coastal strip, which was held by the Philistines. To the north, the powerful Aramaean kingdoms controlled most of central and northern Syria. The remaining Canaanite territory, in the northwest, became Phoenicia. The name derives from the Greek word for "purple", because the Phoenician cities were well known for their technique of purple fabric dyeing (p. 41). There was little farming land in Phoenicia, so the people turned to the sea to make a living, becoming great seafarers and traders. The Phoenicians were also excellent craft workers, and their work was in demand all over the Middle East. Solomon is said to have employed Phoenician workers to build his temple in Jerusalem.

THE LAND OF THE PHOENICIANS
The Phoenicians were based mainly in the cities of Byblos, Sidon, and Tyre, in the coastal area shaded in red on the map.

MUCH-TRAVELLED POT
This elegant painted jug was probably used for perfumed oil. Vessels like this were traded widely throughout the eastern Mediterranean.

Sphinx

Geometric design

MIXED MOTIFS *above*
The much-travelled Phoenicians produced art that blended together a variety of styles. This bronze bowl combines Egyptian sphinxes with North Syrian geometric designs. The overall arrangement is more typical of the Aegean.

FAST MOVER
This Assyrian relief shows a Phoenician ship. It is a bireme, a ship with two banks of oars on either side. Doubling up the oars made the ship fast and effective.

TRADING POST
The Phoenicians are best known as seafarers. Their merchants travelled far from their homeland, and set up colonies around the Mediterranean. The most famous was Carthage, Tunisia, founded in 814 B.C. by settlers from Tyre.

PRECIOUS BOOTY
This piece of carved ivory was used to ornament an item of furniture. It was found at Nimrud, the Assyrian capital, and was probably brought there as tribute (p. 48) or booty from a military campaign.

BRITTLE BUT BEAUTIFUL
Glass-making was one of the most important industries of the Phoenician cities. A paste of finely ground sand mixed with soda was used, and various pigments were added. When fired at a high temperature the mixture fused to form coloured glass.

SHAPING UP
Glass-blowing had not been invented in Phoenician times, so vessels like this were made by moulding the glass paste around a clay core.

Shields

PORT OF CALL
The Phoenicians carried out major engineering projects to transform existing natural harbours into large ports capable of handling the international shipping on which their cities depended. This is a modern view of Byblos, one of their ports.

Double ranks of oars

Inscription reads "Arrowhead of 'Ada', son of Ba'l'a'"

AS EASY AS ABC
The Canaanites probably invented the first alphabet in the Middle Bronze Age. But the Phoenicians refined and developed the system and some of their letters appear on this arrowhead. Their 22-letter alphabet formed the basis of the Greek and ultimately the Roman alphabets.

Gods and goddesses

Until the Israelite concept of the "One God" was widely accepted, religion in the Holy Land involved the worship of a variety of gods and goddesses. These were thought to dominate every aspect of life – war, weather, fertility, the harvest, and so on. Most of what we know about these gods comes from a large archive of clay tablets, dating to the Late Bronze Age, found at the site of Ras Shamra, Syria. These tell us about the supreme god, El, the "father of man", whose domain was the heavens. His wife, Asherah, ruled over the seas. Their children made up a group of over 70 other gods including the storm and warrior god, Baal, and the goddess of love and fertility, Astarte.

EARLY GOD?
The lime-plaster statues from 'Ain Ghazal (p. 9) probably served some ritual function, but whether they were meant to represent gods or their worshippers is unknown.

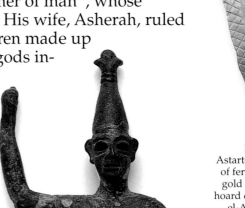

FERTILITY FIGURE
Astarte, the Canaanite goddess of fertility, is depicted on this gold plaque. It comes from a hoard of goldwork found at Tell el-Ajjul, dating to the 16th century B.C.

WARRIOR GOD
This bronze figure, ornamented with silver, dates to the late Bronze Age. It is thought to represent the god Baal, who is depicted as a warrior, brandishing his weapon.

POPULAR DEITY
Perhaps the most powerful and popular Canaanite goddess, Astarte is usually shown naked, with her hands cupping her breasts. This terracotta plaque of Astarte comes from Alalakh.

BAAL'S PROPHETS
King Ahab married Jezebel, a Phoenician princess who reestablished worship of the god Baal in Israel. The prophet Elijah called upon God to light a sacrificial fire in front of the prophets of Baal, to show His superiority.

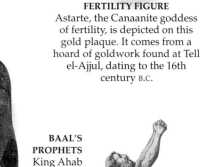

BY THE LIGHT OF THE MOON
This Canaanite temple, excavated at Hazor, was dedicated to the worship of the moon god and his wife.

EGYPTIAN EYE
The eye of Horus was one of the most popular Egyptian amulets (charms). Representing the god Horus in both human and falcon form, it combines a human eye with a falcon's feathers.

WHOSE HAND?
Although many Canaanite temples and shrines have been excavated throughout Palestine, we do not usually know which gods and goddesses were worshipped in them. This finely carved ivory hand was all that remained of the cult statue from the "Fosse" temple at Lachish.

The facade of the temple at Jerusalem depicted on a coin of Simon Bar Kochba

GOD OF WINE
This bust of the Nabataean (Arab) vine god Dushara is from the temple of Dushara at Si'a in the Hauran, southern Syria. It is carved in black basalt, a very hard local stone.

ASTARTE LIVES ON
Despite Israelite religious laws prohibiting the worship of other gods and goddesses, models of Canaanite fertility goddesses, such as Astarte, continued to be produced throughout the Iron Age.

GODS OF EGYPT *left*
The gods of conquering powers were often worshipped alongside the Canaanite gods. Egyptian amulets appeared in the late Bronze Age, when Canaan was ruled by Egypt; they remained popular in the Iron Age. These 9th-century B.C. amulets show the sphinx, with a cat's body and a woman's head, and Sekhmet, goddess of the burning heat of the sun.

Sekhmet   Sekhmet   Sphinx   Sekhmet

GODS OF GREECE
The Greek domination of Syria and Palestine after 332 B.C. brought with it the Greek religion with its various gods and goddesses. Many of these became equated with traditional deities – for example, Aphrodite took on the role of Astarte.

25

Food and crops

PERHAPS THE MOST IMPORTANT advance made by early people was the development of agriculture. It enabled people to settle permanently in one place and to produce more food than they could eat, which in turn stimulated trade and population growth. In the Holy Land, this happened between about 9000 and 6000 B.C., during the final phase of the Stone Age. The process began with the selection of plants and animals that were suitable for cultivation and rearing. Then these species were bred selectively over hundreds of years, gradually becoming suited to the needs of humans (or "domesticated"). Early farmers grew two species of wheat, emmer and einkorn, and also barley. All three crops are native to the Levant. In addition to these cereals, a variety of fruits and vegetables were cultivated.

MILK AND HONEY
Moses' Canaan was indeed a land "flowing with milk and honey", a richly fertile place with a long history of agriculture and horticulture.

FROM THE PHARMACY
Herbs such as cumin were grown not only as flavourings but also for their medicinal value. Cumin was given to treat convulsions. Its oil was also used in perfume.

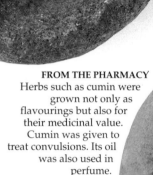

FAVOURED FOR FLAVOUR
The Book of Numbers records how the Israelites of the Exodus remembered with longing the fruits and vegetables they had left behind in Egypt. These included leeks, onions, and garlic. There is every reason to suppose that they would have found these growing in abundance in Canaan too. Even today they are essential in Arabic cooking, and are valued for their distinctive flavourings.

Spring onions

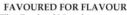

Leeks

THE VERSATILE LENTIL
Lentils were grown from at least the 7th millennium B.C. They could be used in soups, pastes, and purées, or they could be combined with grains and ground into flour to make cakes.

BLOWING IN THE WIND
After harvested cereals had been threshed (beaten to separate out the grains), they were tossed in the air, allowing the lighter chaff to blow away, leaving the heavy grains behind. This process is called "winnowing".

ON THE TERRACES
Terrace agriculture is now common in the Holy Land. This is a comparatively recent form of intensive cultivation on hillside sites.

FOR FOOD AND DRINK
Barley was one of the earliest cereals to be cultivated. It was used to make bread and for brewing beer.

EARLY CROP
Although millet was widely cultivated in Mesopotamia from at least 3000 B.C., it does not seem to have been an important cereal crop in the Holy Land until post-Roman times.

WORKING WITH WHEAT
The grains of the earliest varieties of cultivated wheat, emmer and einkorn, were covered by a tough sheath. This was difficult to remove by threshing. By biblical times, these cereals had been replaced as the main field crop by durum wheat. This species, with its naked grains that were rich in gluten, was easy to thresh and made excellent flour for bread.

Cutting edge

CUTTER
During the first millennium B.C., sickles made of iron came into common usage.

GETTING IN THE HARVEST
Flint blades were set in wooden or bone handles to make sickles for harvesting cereal crops. They often had toothed edges. Developed in the Stone Age, such sickles were used well into the Bronze Age.

27

Continued on next page

THROUGH THE GROVES
This relief from the palace of the Assyrian king Sennacherib at Nineveh shows a group of Chaldean prisoners being led through the palm groves of southern Iraq.

THE GARDEN OF EDEN
The story of the Garden of Eden is illustrated in this painting by Roelandt Jacobsz Savery (1576-1639). The rich variety of the natural world, and the importance of humankind's relationship with the animals and plants, is demonstrated by the story.

FOREIGN FRUIT
In the early days of agriculture, fruit trees were often introduced from neighbouring countries. Apples were probably brought to the Holy Land from Syria or Turkey around 4000 B.C.

SPICE OF LIFE
The Old Testament contains many references to spices. Joseph is said to have been sold by his brothers to Ishmaelite spice-merchants bound for Egypt. Cinnamon, used in cooking and flavouring wine, was imported from India.

MAJOR EXPORT
The olive tree, native to the Syria-Palestine region, became one of its most important natural resources. Olive oil was used in cooking, in medicine, as a base for perfumes, and as a fuel for lamps. It became a major export and was being produced on an industrial scale by the Bronze Age.

Fresh figs

EARLY FRUIT
It is not known where the fig was first cultivated but it was well established in the Holy Land by about 5000 B.C.

Dried figs

Compressed dried figs

STANDBY
Figs were often eaten fresh, but they could also be dried. In this form they could be kept for months, providing a useful reserve food supply in times when other foods were scarce.

POCKET SNACK
Figs could be pressed and made into cakes. Such cakes formed an ideal source of highly nutritious food for long journeys. Perhaps Abraham carried fig cakes on his journey to Canaan from Ur (p. 12).

OIL SPILLAGE
Olive oil was usually kept in large storage jars. But it would have been served at the table in small juglets, like this one from Tell es-Sa'idiyeh, dating to the 12th century B.C.

28

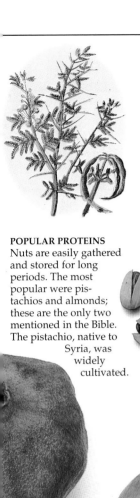

PRIZED SPECIMEN
The acacia or shittim tree is one of the few to grow in the Sinai desert. Acacia wood was used for the Ark of the Covenant described in the Book of Exodus.

POPULAR PROTEINS
Nuts are easily gathered and stored for long periods. The most popular were pistachios and almonds; these are the only two mentioned in the Bible. The pistachio, native to Syria, was widely cultivated.

Pistachios

DATE HARVEST
This relief comes from Tell Halaf (ancient Gozan) in Syria and dates to the 9th century B.C. It shows a man using a ladder to gather dates.

Almonds

PRECIOUS POMEGRANATE
This fruit was prized for its bitter-sweet juice. Its original homes were in Asia Minor, the Caucasus, Armenia, and Persia, but it was certainly established in the Holy Land by the Middle Bronze Age. Examples of the carbonized fruit were found in a tomb at Jericho dating to this period.

The olive seems to have been cultivated from at least 4000 B.C., not only for its delicious fruit but also for its highly prized oil.

FRUIT OF JERICHO
The date palm, which grew abundantly throughout the Fertile Crescent, provided a mainstay of the diet of early people in the area. Jericho is referred to in the Old Testament as the "city of palm trees". The Jericho date was a well-known variety, valued for its succulence.

Continued on next page

Continued from previous page

Fishing

Fish was one of the earliest sources of food, and fishing continued after the development of agriculture, as a useful supplement to the diet. The Assyrians kept supplies of fish in specially made lakes or "vivaria".

HOOKED
This bronze fish hook from Tell es-Sa'idiyeh may have been used for fishing in the River Jordan, which is very close to the site.

FISHERS OF MEN
The importance of fish to the people on the shores of Galilee in Roman times is shown by many biblical stories. The one illustrated here is the miraculous draught of fishes.

MULTI-PURPOSE
Grapes could be dried as raisins like these modern examples. The process goes back at least to the Early Bronze Age and was a useful way of preserving grapes for eating out of season.

Fresh grapes provided a popular and refreshing fruit

Modern white raisins

MASTERS OF WINE
Well-to-do Canaanites of the Late Bronze Age had bronze wine sets made up of a juglet to draw wine from a store-jar, a strainer to filter out any impurities, and a delicate bowl to drink from.

Drinking bowl

Strainer

Juglet

Wine-making

As cities developed in the 3rd millennium B.C., the now large and settled communities of the Levant began to grow additional crops. One of the most important was the grape. Vines had probably been brought in from Anatolia some time during the previous millennium. Now they were widely grown, not only for their fresh fruit, but also for wine-making, and Palestine became renowned for its wines.

SUPPER AT EMAEUS
This painting by Italian artist Caravaggio (1571-1610) reminds us of the importance of mealtimes in early cultures.

ENTER THE CHICKEN
The chicken was domesticated in northern India, some time before 2000 B.C. It was introduced in Egypt by 1400 B.C., but we do not know when it arrived in Palestine. Roast chicken might have been enjoyed by the Israelites, and it was certainly a highly popular food by Roman times.

White cheese, made from cow, goat, or sheep milk, was eaten from at least the Early Bronze Age.

PLATES TO EAT *above*
Circular flaps of unleavened bread were made, as they still are today, by slapping the dough against the inside wall of a simple cylindrical oven, called a tannûr. Such bread flaps could be used as edible platters.

FOWL FOOD
Fowling was probably a less important source of food than hunting or fishing. But these desert partridges, found in the Jordan hills, especially around the Dead Sea, might have provided a change to the diet.

EGGING THEM ON
The eggs of birds, both domestic and wild, were valuable foodstuffs. Ostrich eggs, frequently shown in Egyptian paintings, were especially prized. The hen's eggs shown here are far smaller but also nutritious.

THIRST QUENCHER
The water melon was widely grown in ancient Egypt and was probably eaten in Palestine from at least the beginning of the Middle Bronze Age (about 2000 B.C.). It was prized as a source of water during dry periods.

Water melon seeds could be eaten as a food

WHISKED AWAY
This unusual bronze object was found in the "Fosse Temple" at Lachish. But it was not used in temple rituals. Its similarity to modern Arab utensils shows that it was simply a food whisk.

It is not known when cucumbers were introduced into Palestine, but it was probably during the 2nd millennium B.C., by which time they were a common food in Egypt.

Ancient Canaanite vessel

31

Animals

The scarab beetle was held sacred by the Egyptians; their seals were often made in the shape of scarabs

Jesus as the "Good Shepherd" from a 19th-century engraving

Today the Holy Land boasts a rich variety of wildlife, including about 100 species of mammal. Many that were once present have now disappeared. Lions, bears, ostriches, and crocodiles, all mentioned in the Bible, have been hunted to extinction. Archaeozoologists are people who study ancient animals, recording and analysing animal bones found at excavations. Their work can tell us much about the changing relationship between humankind and the animal kingdom. Before the development of agriculture (pp. 26-27), animals were hunted for food and skins. With the advent of stock-rearing, people began to use animals for other products, such as wool and dairy produce. The first animals to be domesticated in this way, during the Stone Age, were sheep and goats. In the following Chalcolithic period, pigs and cattle were being reared too.

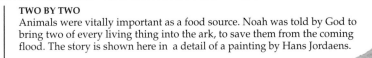

TWO BY TWO
Animals were vitally important as a food source. Noah was told by God to bring two of every living thing into the ark, to save them from the coming flood. The story is shown here in a detail of a painting by Hans Jordaens.

Hollow snout, indicating that this vessel may have been a feeding bottle

POPULAR PLAYTHING *left*
Model animals were popular toys in ancient times, just as they are today. This Iron-Age pottery cow from Lachish might have been such a plaything. It could also have been a feeding bottle, since it has a hole in the top and a hollow snout to drink through.

WILD ONE
The shy Nubian ibex or beden is the "wild goat" of the Bible. It is still found in some rocky areas today.

MONKEY BUSINESS
This amulet shows an ape. Such creatures were imported from Africa in Solomon's reign.

WHAT, A BOAR?
Wild boars, like the one on this amulet from Lachish, can still be found in the thickets that line the Jordan valley.

SAMPSON AND THE LION
In Old Testament times the lion was common in Palestine and often posed a threat to humans and their stock.

BEARS IN THE WOODS
Small, pale-coated Syrian bears lived in Palestine until quite recently. In biblical times they lived in hilly, wooded areas.

SPOTTED IN THE CLIFFS
Leopards were common in Palestine in biblical times – and long after. One was seen in the cliffs at En Gedi as recently as 1974.

PAYMENT TO THE KING
The Black Obelisk is a monument put up in Nimrud to commemorate 31 military campaigns of the Assyrian king Shalmaneser III. This detail from the obelisk shows some of the tribute paid to the king by the ruler of Sukha in Syria. It depicts two lions and a deer, animals native to the middle Euphrates area. The artist could not have seen many lions since he has given them jackal tails!

OUT FOR A DUCK
The duck was a popular source of food and was often a subject for artists. This ivory duck from Lachish was probably the decorative end of a cosmetic spoon.

IN THE STABLE
The importance of meat- and milk-producing animals is shown by the presence of such creatures in engravings like this nativity by Gustave Doré (1832-83).

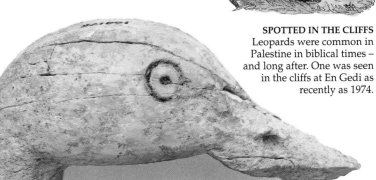

THREE WISE MEN
The wise men ride one-humped Arabian camels, which were domesticated in Egypt before 3000 B.C. and were familiar in Palestine by 1500 B.C. Two-humped Bactrian camels appeared during the Iron Age.

Clothing

Because items like textiles are only occasionally preserved, archaeologists have to rely on paintings, sculptures, and models for their evidence of what people wore in the earliest times. The earliest people probably clothed themselves in animal skins. But spinning and weaving do date back to at least the 7th millennium B.C., as shown by a remarkable discovery of preserved organic material at Nahal Hemar in the Judean Desert. Some equipment for making cloth also survives, to give us further clues. Later people wore clothes made of a variety of materials, and these were often brightly coloured with natural dyes. Leather and felt were also important materials, for shoes and hats as well as clothes.

HIGH AND MIGHTY
Clothing could show social status. This rich woman of the 10th century B.C. wears an elaborate headdress.

EGYPTIAN INFLUENCE
The well-travelled Phoenicians had an excellent knowledge of the costumes of many countries. A Phoenician carved this ivory panel showing a figure wearing royal Egyptian-style garments.

TOOLS FOR THE LOOM
It is not always clear how these bone weaving tools were used. The spatula was probably slipped between the vertical warp threads on the loom and forced upwards to close up the horizontal weft threads.

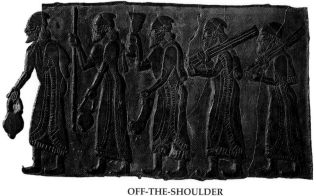

OFF-THE-SHOULDER
These Israelites wear skull caps, long kilts, and cloaks draped over one shoulder, leaving the other shoulder exposed. The kilts and cloaks are shown fringed and they were probably woven in brightly coloured patterns.

LOOM WEIGHT *below*
Often made of unbaked clay, these were used to weigh down the vertical warp threads of the loom.

Point or awl

Spatula

REBEKAH
This is a painting of Rebekah, wife of Isaac in the Book of Genesis, at the well. It illustrates the 19th-century idea of costume in Old Testament times.

IN A SPIN *above*
In the process of spinning, fibres are twisted together to make a continuous thread. To do this people used a stick with a type of "fly wheel" on it to give it momentum. These objects are called "spindle whorls", and are often found on excavations in the Holy Land.

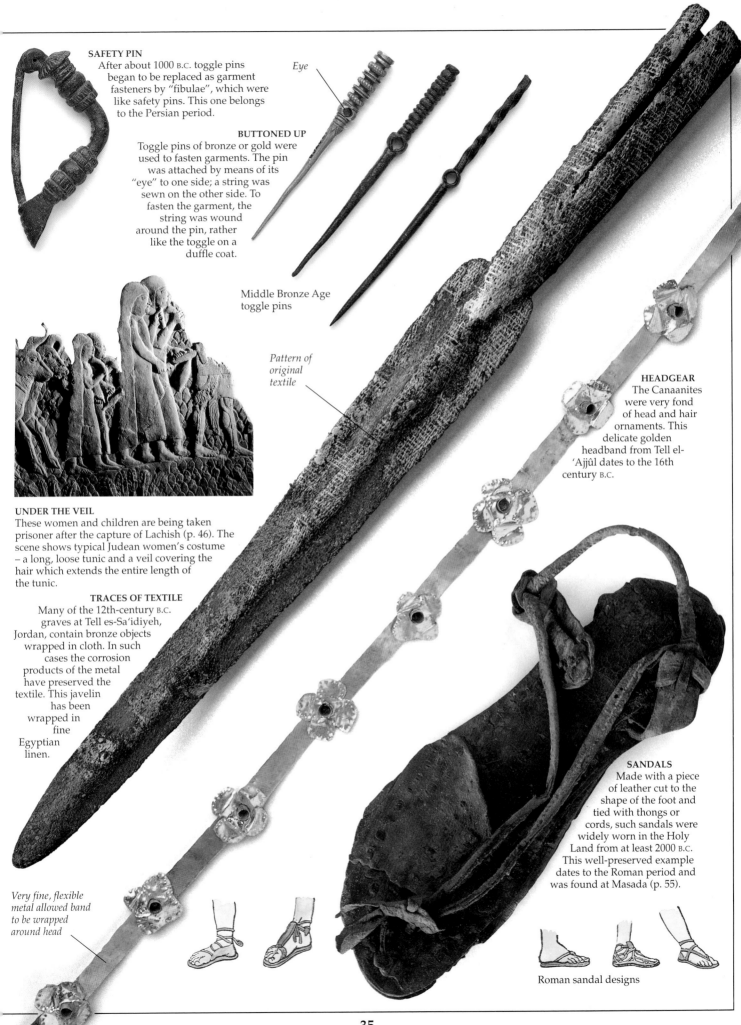

SAFETY PIN
After about 1000 B.C. toggle pins began to be replaced as garment fasteners by "fibulae", which were like safety pins. This one belongs to the Persian period.

Eye

BUTTONED UP
Toggle pins of bronze or gold were used to fasten garments. The pin was attached by means of its "eye" to one side; a string was sewn on the other side. To fasten the garment, the string was wound around the pin, rather like the toggle on a duffle coat.

Middle Bronze Age toggle pins

Pattern of original textile

HEADGEAR
The Canaanites were very fond of head and hair ornaments. This delicate golden headband from Tell el-'Ajjûl dates to the 16th century B.C.

UNDER THE VEIL
These women and children are being taken prisoner after the capture of Lachish (p. 46). The scene shows typical Judean women's costume – a long, loose tunic and a veil covering the hair which extends the entire length of the tunic.

TRACES OF TEXTILE
Many of the 12th-century B.C. graves at Tell es-Sa'idiyeh, Jordan, contain bronze objects wrapped in cloth. In such cases the corrosion products of the metal have preserved the textile. This javelin has been wrapped in fine Egyptian linen.

SANDALS
Made with a piece of leather cut to the shape of the foot and tied with thongs or cords, such sandals were widely worn in the Holy Land from at least 2000 B.C. This well-preserved example dates to the Roman period and was found at Masada (p. 55).

Very fine, flexible metal allowed band to be wrapped around head

Roman sandal designs

Gold earrings of the Roman period from Lachish

Jewellery

THE NEED TO ADORN the body using jewellery and cosmetics must have been felt from the very earliest times. Such decorations could be used to show the wearer's social status or wealth, or to express religious beliefs. Simple beads and pendants of bone, shell, and stone are often found in prehistoric burials. The value placed on such items is clear from the amount of skill and time that went into their manufacture. These materials were used long after the techniques of gold and silver working had been learned. In the hands of the Canaanite craftsmen of the Middle and Late Bronze Ages jewellery became a highly accomplished art form. The goldwork displays sophisticated techniques such as repoussée (raising the surface in relief by hammering from behind) and granulation (the use of tiny grains of metal). The Israelites did not learn these skills. But they were inherited by the Phoenicians, whose jewellery was widely sought-after.

SILVER GRAINS
This Iron-Age silver earring has fine granulated decoration.

HOLLOW GOLD
From the Persian period, this gold earring is made up of hollow spheres.

HAIR DRESSING
The finest hair combs were made of bone or ivory, and were often ornamented with finely carved geometric or naturalistic designs.

FOR FACE PAINTING
During the Early Bronze Age, hollowed-out and finely engraved animal bones were used as containers for cosmetics such as eye make-up.

PENDANTS
These unusual bone pendants from Lachish, dating to the Iron Age, probably had some significance in addition to being decorative. The varying numbers of dot and circle motifs suggests that some might have served as calendars or reckoners. Another suggestion is that a group of such pendants would be unstrung and thrown on the ground, and the resulting pattern used for looking into the future.

Lengths of beaten bronze could be easily bent to the right size

Bangles and anklets were a popular form of jewellery in the Iron-Age.

THREADING THEM THROUGH *above*
Like most Canaanite necklaces, this one was found without its original thread. The arrangement of the beads is therefore quite arbitrary.

Faience bead

BEAUTIFUL BLUES *above*
During the Late Bronze Age, many beads were made of faience. This is a blue glazed material consisting mainly of quartz.

HOLY OFFERING
In the "Fosse Temple", a Late Bronze Age Canaanite sanctuary at Lachish, a number of gold pendants were found. They probably formed part of an offering to the deity.

Decoration formed by impression made when gold is beaten over a patterned object

TOUCH OF GLAMOUR
Jewellery worn by actress Vivien Leigh in her role as Cleopatra was based on Middle Eastern originals. Notice the headband and jewelled earrings.

Traces of linen

EGYPTIAN PLANTS
Many Late Bronze Age beads and pendants show strong Egyptian influence. The palmettes on this necklace are a typical motif.

Palmette

BELOW THE BELT
The lower part of an Iron Age terracotta figure clearly shows two pairs of anklets of the type shown opposite.

FISH OUT OF WATER
Towards the end of the Late Bronze Age, many objects made in Egypt were imported into Canaan. This fine ivory cosmetic box in the shape of a fish was found inside the bronze bowl in an unusual 12th-century B.C. grave at Tell es-Sa'idiyeh. The bowl had been strapped over the genitals of the deceased using Egyptian linen, traces of which still remain.

Money and trade

Found at Amathus in Cyprus, this Phoenician glass vessel was probably used to hold incense

THE HOLY LAND is at the heart of the fertile crescent (p. 10). This made it a corridor for international traders. Merchants travelled between Egypt and Arabia in the south, Anatolia and Mesopotamia in the north; there was also maritime trade with the Mediterranean islands. These contacts go back a long way. In the Neolithic period there was trade in obsidian, a black volcanic glass that was used to make tools. But it was the growth of cities in the third millennium B.C. that really laid the foundations for the trade that would sustain the civilizations of the area for thousands of years. In Palestine, farming developed so that surpluses of cereals, flour, oil, and wine could be exported to foreign markets. Canaanite art and craft objects were also exported widely. In return, raw materials such as wood and metal came in from abroad.

WEIGHING THEM UP
Before coins were invented, commercial deals were done using a variety of materials. Metal ingots or scraps were often used as a currency of established value and these had to be weighed so that their worth could be assessed. So accurate weights were needed, like these lion-shaped ones from Assyria. They are inscribed with the name of King Shalmaneser III, for whom they were made.

During their first revolt against Rome in A.D. 66 (p. 55), the Jews struck their own coins

WAGON TRAIN
A pottery model of a covered wagon from Hamman in Syria shows the type of vehicle that was used to transport goods in the late 3rd millennium B.C. Wagons like this might have been used by travelling metalworkers, peddling their wares from town to town.

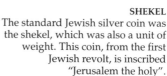

SHEKEL
The standard Jewish silver coin was the shekel, which was also a unit of weight. This coin, from the first Jewish revolt, is inscribed "Jerusalem the holy".

STOPPING ON THE WAY
This detail of an evocative painting by Edward Lear (1812-88) shows a desert caravan stopping by Mount Sinai. It gives a good idea of what long-distance caravan traffic must have been like in ancient times.

ROMAN CASH
Coins came into common use in the Holy Land at the time of the conquest of Alexander (p. 54). Roman imperial coins bore a portrait of the emperor, in this case, Vespasian.

ONE HUMP OR TWO?
Two-humped Bactrian camels appear on the Assyrian Black Obelisk (p.33). These creatures did not appear in the Holy Land until Solomon's time. Before this, trading caravans relied on the one-humped Arabian camel.

A coin of the second Jewish revolt (A.D. 132-135) bears the name of its leader Shimeon

MAN OF THE PEOPLE?
These bronze coins are from the reign of Herod's son Archelaus (4 B.C.–A.D. 6). One shows a crested helmet, the other a bunch of grapes. The Greek inscription reads "Herod, governor of the people".

Because coins circulated widely, they had a propaganda value. These two from the second Jewish revolt bear inscriptions. The first reads "Year one of the redemption of Israel", the second bears the name of the leader Shimeon.

POPPY POWER
During the Late Bronze Age little jugs, known as "bil-bils" were imported into Canaan. Analysis of substances found inside some of them has shown that they were used to hold the drug opium. The shape of the jug is strikingly like that of an upturned poppy head.

39

Continued on next page

A bronze coin of Agrippa I (A.D. 37-44), grandson of Herod the Great. He used the parasol as a symbol of monarchy.

INSTEAD OF MONEY
Precious metals were frequently traded as ingots. This silver ingot is from Zinjirli, ancient Sam'al.

TURNING THE TABLES
Jesus of Nazareth objected to merchants trading their wares in the precincts of the Temple in Jerusalem, and overthrew the stalls and tables.

COMMEMORATION
Coins could be made to commemorate famous events. This coin inscribed "Judaea Capta" records the Roman victory in the first Jewish revolt (p. 55).

Handles of this shape give this vessel the name "stirrup jar"

IMPORT
Beautifully made and elegantly decorated, Mycenean vessels known as "stirrup jars" were imported into Canaan during the Late Bronze Age, perhaps containing perfumed oils.

MERCHANT SHIP OF SOLOMON'S FLEET
King Solomon was intent upon developing a wide network of sea trade relations. With the co-operation of Hiram, king of Tyre, he built a major port at Ezion Geber at the head of the Red Sea. A joint Israelite and Phoenician fleet was based here, and every three years, ships set sail for "Ophir" (probably the Somali coast of East Africa), in search of fine gold.

STORE JAR
In the 12th century B.C., Tell es-Sa'idiyeh, on the eastern side of the river Jordan, was an Egyptian taxation and distribution centre, collecting produce from Transjordan for shipment to Egypt. Jars of Egyptian design were found in one of the storerooms at the site and may have been used to store and transport wine.

SEA HORSES
Timber was always a valuable item of trade. The most expensive and sought-after wood came from the "Cedars of Lebanon". This 8th-century B.C. Assyrian relief shows Phoenician merchant ships hauling logs along the Syrian coast. These ships were called hippoi, meaning horses, as they had horse figureheads.

8 Shekels

"Neseph", five-sixths of a shekel

"Beqa'", half a shekel

HOW HEAVY?
The ancient Palestinian system of weights was based on the shekel (equivalent to about 11.4 g), the mina (60 shekels) and the kikkar or "talent" (60 minas). These stone weights are inscribed in Hebrew with their value.

LONG-DISTANCE TRADER *above*
This Roman merchant ship, known as a corbita, has two masts, and sails made of oblong blocks of cloth sewn together and reinforced with leather patches at the corners. Such vessels were used for long-distance shipping across the Mediterranean rather than for coastal use.

LIGHTING THE WAY
Pharos, the lighthouse of Alexandria, the port city and capital of Egypt founded by Alexander the Great, was one of the seven wonders of the ancient world.

ROYAL PURPLE
One of the most sought-after items traded by Phoenician merchants was their purple-dyed cloth. By the time of the Roman Empire, its prestige was so great that it could only be worn by the emperor.

THEIR TRUE COLOURS
The highly prized purple dye for which the Phoenicians are renowned was extracted from a gland of the murex snail. Each snail yielded only a drop of yellow liquid which darkened on exposure to light. Processing required slow simmering for about two weeks. Up to 60,000 snails were needed for each pound of dye. Different tints were achieved by varying the amount of extract from different species.

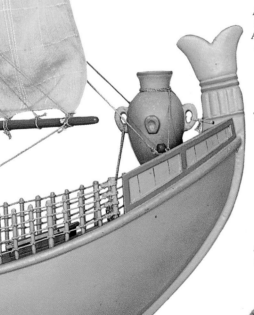

Arts and crafts

SOME OF THE EARLIEST PEOPLE of the Holy Land were skilled in the arts and crafts, producing items of beauty for religious purposes and as status symbols. Those who made the lime-plaster statues found at 'Ain Ghazal (pp. 8-9) in the Stone Age had great expertise. They also displayed great refinement in the way they applied the decoration to the statues. Wonderfully carved ivories and elaborate copper objects are found in the following Chalcolithic period. But it was the Canaanites of the Bronze Age and the Phoenicians of the Iron Age who turned this tradition of skilful work into a real industry, producing works of art and craft that were much admired and sought after throughout the eastern Mediterranean and beyond.

FOR SHOW
In the Middle Bronze Age, metal-casting techniques became more and more sophisticated. This bronze axe-head, decorated with a lion fighting a dog, was probably for ceremonial use.

Incised alphabetic writing

MUSIC MAKERS
Dancing and music were undoubtedly popular activities throughout the history of Palestine, although few instruments have survived. Written descriptions and pictures suggest that a wide variety of instruments, such as harps, lyres, flutes, trumpets, and a range of percussion instruments, were used.

WRITING IT DOWN
The art of writing using alphabetic letters was begun by the Canaanites (pp. 16-17). One of the earliest attempts at alphabetic script was found on this 17th-century B.C. bronze dagger from Lachish.

DAILY LIFE IN ANCIENT JERICHO
Wooden furniture was preserved in some of the tombs in Jericho. Canaanite carpenters had an extensive tool kit. They put their products together using accurate joints and decorated them with carving.

IVORY QUEENS
The Canaanites and Phoenicians were renowned for their ivory carving. This material was often used for inlays or ornaments for furniture. Sometimes they have letters on the back to show where they should be attached. This example is a 9th-century Phoenician ivory from the Assyrian city of Nimrud. It shows two seated queens in Egyptian style and was decorated with blue glass and gold overlay.

HARD TO CARVE
The combat between a lion and a dog seems to have been a popular subject for the Canaanites. This example is carved on a piece of black basalt, a very hard stone which took great skill to work. It dates to the 14th century B.C. and comes from Beth Shan.

Applied gold decoration

SYRIAN STYLE
This ivory female head was found at Nimrud. Its style of carving lacks the sophistication of the Phoenician piece opposite. It might have been the work of a Syrian carver.

Most of the methods of the ancient potter are still used today. Here a village potter in Egypt produces simple domestic wares

FUNNY FACE
The finest pottery ever seen in Palestine, both in terms of technical quality and beauty, was made by the Canaanites. Their potters also had a sense of humour, as shown by this extraordinary face vase from Jericho, dating to the 6th century B.C.

GOLDEN GRAINS
This fine pendant comes from Tell el-'Ajjûl and dates to the 16th century B.C. It is decorated by granulation. In this process gold wire is melted to make tiny beads, which are then soldered to the surface.

Granulation

CARVED IN STONE
Vessels carved from stones such as calcite and alabaster were extremely popular in the Late Bronze and Iron Ages, perhaps as containers for perfumed oil. This example comes from Tell es-Sa'idiyeh.

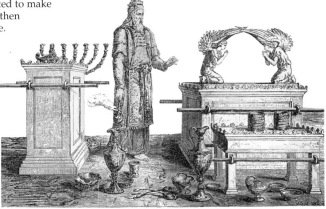

TREASURES OF THE TEMPLE
When the Egyptians left Canaan they took the best artists and craftsmen. So Solomon asked the king of Tyre for Phoenician artisans when building his Temple in Jerusalem. Phoenician metalworkers probably made the temple furnishings mentioned in the Bible and shown in this old engraving.

War and weapons

This relief shows an Aramaean cavalryman of the 9th century B.C. It comes from Tell Halaf, the biblical Gozan.

FROM THE EARLIEST TIMES weapons were used for hunting and to protect people against their enemies. Until copper smelting was invented some time before 4000 B.C., the people of the Holy Land made weapons out of wood, bone, and stone. As the Early Bronze Age cities grew, the techniques of warfare developed and armies were established. The more advanced metalworking of this period provided soldiers with mass-produced swords, spears, and axes. Initially these were made of copper, later of bronze. Later in the Bronze Age war and weapons became more sophisticated, with field battles involving cavalry and chariots; well-defended cities were attacked using special siege equipment. The Philistines probably introduced ironworking into Canaan around 1200 B.C; after this, iron weapons gradually replaced bronze ones.

Pair of helmets from the Persian period

GIANT-SLAYER
One of the most ancient of all weapons was the sling. Because they were made of leather or cloth, few examples have survived, but groups of slingshots (either shaped "bullets" of clay or smooth, rounded pebbles) are frequently found. The Bible recounts how David killed the Philistine leader Goliath using a sling – a most plausible story given the deadly accuracy of this powerful weapon.

TAKING AIM
This slinger is depicted on a 9th-century B.C. relief from the royal palace at Tell Halaf (Gozan), Syria.

GOOD GRIP
The hilt of this Late Bronze Age dagger from Alalakh in Syria was cast with deep recesses to allow a wooden or bone grip to be inserted.

Broad cutting blade

Sword would have been attached to wooden or bone hilt with copper rivets

Ridge to make blade stronger

Axe

Sickle sword

Shield

SOCKETED SPEAR
During the Middle Bronze Age, improved casting techniques made it possible to make spear and javelin heads with a hollow socket to take a shaft.

Socket

AXE-MAN
This bronze warrior figure of the Middle Bronze Age holds a distinctive axe with a head shaped rather like a duck's bill. The figure with its "duckbill" axe was found in the early part of this period (about 1800 B.C.)

ARMED TO THE TEETH
This Middle Bronze Age warrior holds a spear and a "sickle sword", a type of weapon now known from several examples found in sites in both Canaan and Egypt. A sickle sword is shown being carried by one of the Canaanites on the Egyptian Beni Hasan wall paintings (pp. 10-11).

Tang for attaching to shaft

KEEPING IT ALL TOGETHER
Early Bronze Age copper javelins with long "tangs" were tightly lashed to their wooden shafts with leather thongs.

This archer has a composite bow, a powerful weapon made of layers of wood, glue, horn, and sinew.

LEGIONARY
During the Roman period, a highly organized army helped the emperors keep control of their vast territories. This soldier holds the standard of his legion.

HORSEPOWER
The Canaanites used two-horse chariots as light and fast fighting vehicles. This later Greek chariot was drawn by four horses.

Thin blade, suitable for stabbing

HEAVYWEIGHT WEAPON
During the final phase of the Early Bronze Age (the time of the patriarchs, pp. 10-11), city life in Canaan declined, and the population moved into the countryside. Metal weapons became larger and heavier, more suited to the harsher conditions this change in lifestyle entailed. This sword from Beit Dagin, near Tel-Aviv, is one of the largest known weapons of this period.

Continued on next page

The siege of Lachish

The northern kingdom of Israel came to an end in 722 B.C. with the capture of Samaria by the Assyrians. The southern kingdom of Judah was also forced to submit to the might of the Assyrians, and although Hezekiah (715-687/6 B.C.) rebelled against the Assyrian king Sennacherib in 704 B.C., the attempt was a disaster. In 701 B.C. Sennacherib swept into Judah and destroyed many cities, including Lachish. The siege and capture of this city are vividly depicted in a series of limestone reliefs from Sennacherib's palace at Nineveh. The Assyrians finally advanced on Jerusalem, where Hezekiah was forced to submit and pay heavy tribute.

Flaming torches thrown down by the defenders

MIGHTY MAN
This painting by 19th-century artist William Dyce shows Joash, son of Shemaah of Gibesh, who was one of David's heroes.

ARROWHEADS
When bronze became freely available after 2000 B.C., arrow-heads made of the metal were used widely. Iron arrowheads came in after about 1100 B.C.

Broken ladder – used by the Assyrians for scaling but pushed down by the defenders

Selection of bronze arrowheads

DOWN WITH THE WALLS
The battering ram may have been developed as early as the Middle Bronze Age. It continued to provide an effective way of attacking defensive walls until the advent of explosives.

Battering ram – the soldier at the front is pouring water over the front of the machine to prevent it catching fire

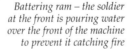

Iron arrowhead

TORTOISE SHELL
The Romans used stout swords and big rectangular shields. In close formations, especially when attacking cities, soldiers would lock their shields to-gether to form a solid wall or roof. This formation was known as a *testudo* or tortoise.

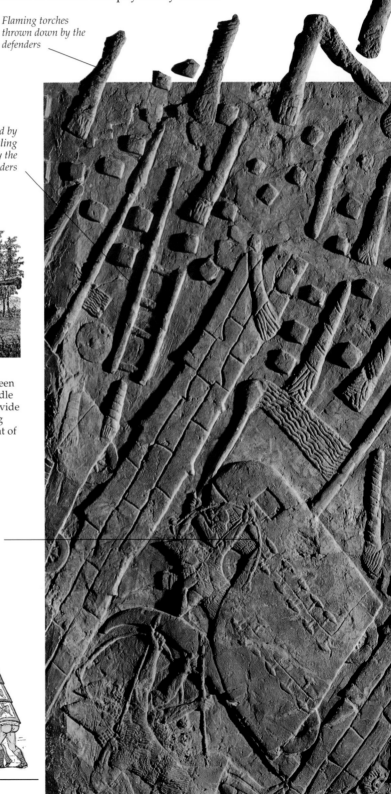

BETTER BATTLE AXES
During the period of the patriarchs, towards the end of the third millennium B.C., battle axes were developed that could be secured to the handle by means of a socket. They were highly effective in piercing metal helmets – and cracking skulls!

Axehead with handle

DUCK'S BILL
During the Middle Bronze Age, axe blades were made longer, to produce the so-called "duck-billed" axe.

Parapet of round shields on top of city gatehouse

Judaean archers and slingers defending the gatehouse

Large hooded shield

Assryian archer – the pointed helmet was effective protection against vertically falling showers of arrows

Assyrian spearman with crested helmet

Siege ramps of banked-up earth covered with logs

Deportees leaving the gate, bound for exile in Assyria, carrying with them a few possessions in bags

Bronze scale armour like this was worn by the Assyrians during the siege of Lachish

A 19th-century impression of scale armour

This Roman catapult could hurl rocks over long distances. It was called an *onager* (wild ass) because of its kicking action.

The Assyrians

THE KINGDOM OF ASSYRIA was centred on the valley of the River Tigris in northern Iraq. It had existed since at least 2000 B.C. During the 9th century B.C., the Assyrian kings began to expand their territory, both to secure their boundaries and to gain control of trade routes. The next 200 years saw the relentless advance of the Assyrian armies in regular campaigns against Syria, Phoenicia, and ultimately Israel and Judah. The kings of these states could buy a little time by paying tribute to the Assyrians – taxes in the form of treasures or other goods – but failure to meet the increasing demands, or any form of resistance, was met by crushing retaliation. Territories conquered by the Assyrians were added to the growing empire. In 722 B.C. the northern kingdom of Israel effectively came to an end with the taking of its capital, Samaria, and the loss of part of its population through the Assyrian policy of moving people from their homelands. Judah survived longer, but only by paying crippling tribute. Many of the exploits of the Assyrians are shown on carved stone slabs made to adorn the royal palaces.

HOUSEHOLD GOD
The Assyrians often placed figures of gods beneath the floors of their houses and palaces, to keep out evil demons. This one is the god Lahmu, "the hairy".

HEROIC STRUGGLE
In spite of their warlike image, the Assyrians greatly appreciated art and fine craftsmanship. This carved ivory plaque shows a hero or king fighting a lion. It was made locally in Assyria.

THE EMPIRE'S SPREAD
At its greatest extent, in the early 7th century B.C., the Assyrian Empire covered a vast area, stretching from Iran to Egypt.

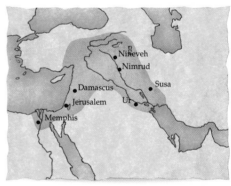

Bottle

WAR GODDESS
This bronze plaque shows Ishtar, the most important goddess of the Assyrians. Here she is depicted as the goddess of war, carrying arms and mounted on her favoured animal, the lion. Ishtar was the equivalent of the Canaanite goddess Astarte (pp. 24-25).

FOR HOME AND PALACE
These two vessels show the skill and artistry of the Assyrian potter. The elegant, thin-walled beaker on the left is an example of "Assyrian palace ware". On the right is a small bottle, beautifully decorated in multi-coloured glaze. Both pieces date to the 8th-7th centuries B.C.

Beaker

TRIBUTE FROM PHOENICIA
Carved ivories were often used to decorate furniture. This panel from the Assyrian capital, Nimrud, showing a woman wearing an Egyptian-style wig, was made by a Phoenician craftsman. It was probably brought back in the 8th century B.C. from one of the western campaigns as part of war booty or tribute.

GODDESS OF LOVE
This blue plaque showing a winged goddess comes from the temple of Ninurta at Nimrud. It dates to the 9th century B.C. The goddess is probably Ishtar, shown in her guise as goddess of love.

Blue colour typical of Assyrian decorative wares

PAYMENTS TO THE KING
The military campaigns of the Assyrian king Shalmaneser III (858-824 B.C.) were commemorated on a stone monument, now known as the Black Obelisk, which was set up in the capital, Nimrud. One of the scenes shows Jehu, king of Israel, giving tribute to Shalmaneser. The kneeling figure may not be Jehu himself, but a representative. The tribute itself is shown on another panel.

LION'S SHARE
Lions were a popular subject in Assyrian art. This one might originally have been attached to the handle of a fan.

MAKING YOUR MARK
Small stone cylinders with a hole through them were carved with a design and rolled out on clay tablets or jar or parcel sealings. The resulting impression acted as a signature or mark of ownership. This chalcedony seal, dating to around 750 B.C., shows a heroic figure grasping two ostriches by the neck.

STATE ROOM
The richly decorated throne room of King Ashurnasirpal II at Nimrud is shown here reconstructed by a 19th-century artist. The carved reliefs, which today are seen as plain stone, were originally brightly painted.

49

The Babylonians

Hebrew seal of the Neo-Babylonian period

Mesopotamia, the land between the Rivers Tigris and Euphrates in what is now Iraq, was one of the earliest centres of civilization in the Middle East. At the start of the 2nd millennium B.C., the Amorites, a people originally from the Syrian desert, founded a dynasty at the city of Babylon on the Euphrates. In the 18th century B.C., under King Hammurabi, the Babylonians achieved supremacy over the whole of Mesopotamia, establishing an empire that stretched from Mari in the northwest to Elam in the east. This "Old Babylonian" period was brought to an end by the Hittite King Mursilis I, who attacked Babylonia in 1595 B.C. and destroyed the city of Babylon. In the 7th century B.C., the city's fortunes improved, when a local official of Chaldean descent, Nabopolassar, took control of southern Mesopotamia, and assumed kingship of Babylon, founding the Chaldean or Neo-Babylonian dynasty.

NABOPOLASSAR'S EMPIRE
In 612 B.C., Nabopolassar overthrew the Assyrians and laid claim to their lands including Judah. His son Nebuchadnezzar raided Judah in 597 B.C. after a rebellion. When revolt broke out again ten years later, Nebuchadnezzar responded with a devastating campaign which destroyed Jerusalem.

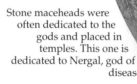

Stone maceheads were often dedicated to the gods and placed in temples. This one is dedicated to Nergal, god of disease

BUILDER
Bronze figures showing a king carrying a basket filled with building materials were placed in the foundations of temples. The inscription gives the names of the king and the god of the temple.

AGE OF AQUARIUS
The Babylonians are thought to have invented the zodiac. This terracotta plaque shows a giant carrying streams of water – the ancestor of Aquarius.

GREAT GATE
Nebuchadnezzar rebuilt Babylon. One of the most impressive buildings was the Ishtar Gate, which gave access to the processional road leading to the main temple.

TOWER OR TEMPLE? *right*
According to the book of Genesis, the Tower of Babel was built by the descendants of Noah in order to reach Heaven. This is a reference to Babylon's ziggurat or temple-tower. This depiction of the tower is from a detail of a painting by Pieter Bruegel the elder (1525-69).

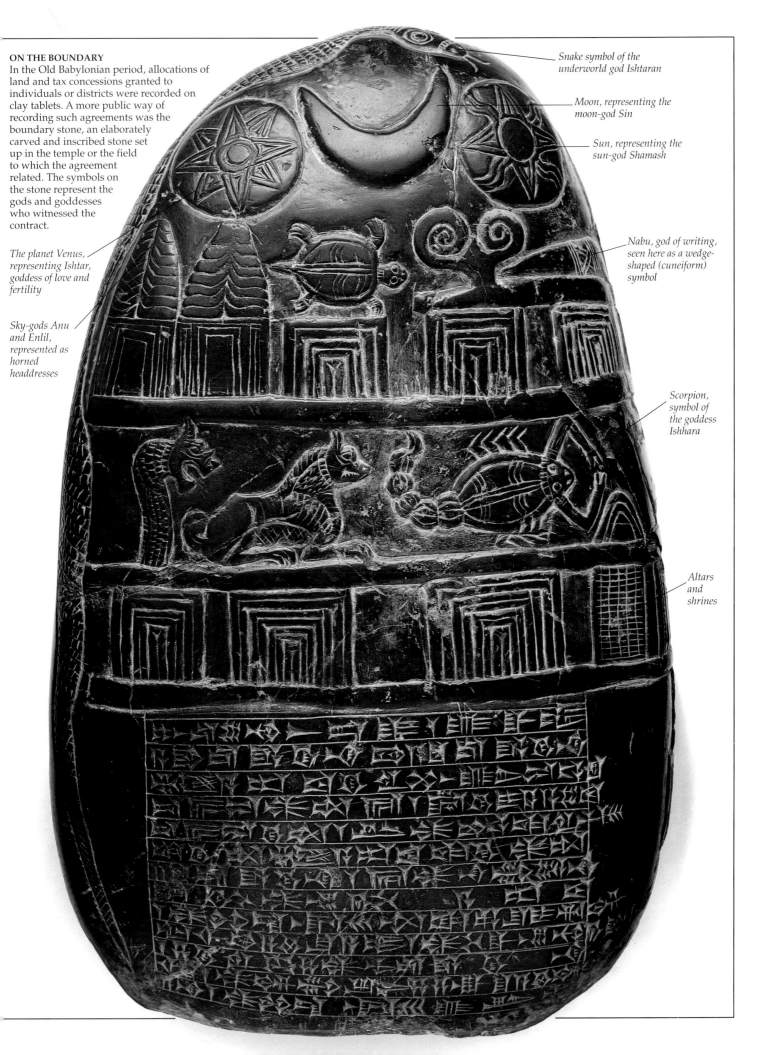

ON THE BOUNDARY
In the Old Babylonian period, allocations of land and tax concessions granted to individuals or districts were recorded on clay tablets. A more public way of recording such agreements was the boundary stone, an elaborately carved and inscribed stone set up in the temple or the field to which the agreement related. The symbols on the stone represent the gods and goddesses who witnessed the contract.

The planet Venus, representing Ishtar, goddess of love and fertility

Sky-gods Anu and Enlil, represented as horned headdresses

Snake symbol of the underworld god Ishtaran

Moon, representing the moon-god Sin

Sun, representing the sun-god Shamash

Nabu, god of writing, seen here as a wedge-shaped (cuneiform) symbol

Scorpion, symbol of the goddess Ishhara

Altars and shrines

The Persians

ORIGINALLY FROM TURKESTAN, the Persians moved into western Iran during the second millennium B.C. and settled in Parsa (now Fars). Their early history is closely linked to that of the Medes, who settled in the same region. In alliance with the Babylonians, the Medes, under their king Cyaxeres, overthrew the Assyrian state in 612 B.C. In 550 B.C. Cyrus of the house of Achaemenes deposed his grandfather, the Median king Astyages, and became undisputed ruler of both Medes and Persians. The Achaemenid empire was born, and went from strength to strength. Soon Cyrus had added much of western Anatolia to his territories. In 539 B.C. he defeated Babylonia, inheriting its empire, which included Syria and Palestine. It was during the reign of Cyrus that the Jews were allowed to return to Palestine. The rebuilding of Jerusalem and its temple are described in the Books of Ezra and Nehemiah.

Wealthy or important people sewed ornaments like this on to their clothes.

THE ACHAEMENID EMPIRE
At its maximum extent during the reign of Darius I (522-486 B.C.), the empire stretched from Egypt and Libya in the west to the Indus River in the east.

ROYAL CENTRE
Persepolis was an important civic and religious centre built by Darius I and his successor Xerxes (486-465 B.C.). It is shown here in an imaginative 19th-century reconstruction.

GLAMOROUS GOAT
This silver goat is said to come from Persepolis and dates to the 5th century B.C.

ON GUARD
This Persian palace guard is portrayed on a glazed brick frieze from Susa.

Cuneiform (wedge-shaped) script

LION AT BAY
A royal lion hunt is portrayed on this impression of an agate cylinder seal. The inscription records the name "Darius the Great King", probably Darius I (522-486 B.C.).

Ahuramazda, the supreme god of the Persians

FINERY FROM AFAR
The Persian kings employed artists and craftsmen of many nationalities, and foreign influence can be seen in many of their works of art. The applied golden figures on this silver bowl show a winged lion with the head of the Egyptian dwarf god Bes, wearing a feathered crown.

Spout to take wick

LIGHT ON THE SUBJECT
Dating to the 6th century B.C., this bronze lamp was found in the "Solar shrine" at Lachish, a small temple associated with sun worship.

HIGH CEREMONY
This imaginative reconstruction shows one of the ceremonies that might have taken place at Persepolis.

CYRUS CYLINDER
The text on this clay cylinder tells how Cyrus allowed people in captivity in Babylon to return to their homelands. It does not mention the Jews, but it was this policy that allowed them to return to Palestine.

The Greeks and Romans

AFTER THE BATTLE OF ISSUS in 332 B.C., the vast empire of the Persians fell into the hands of the Macedonian ruler Alexander the Great. When Alexander died nine years later, Palestine first came under the control of his general Ptolemy and his descendants, then passed to the rule of the Seleucids, a dynasty based in Syria. In 167 B.C., the Seleucid Antiochus IV sacked and looted the Temple in Jerusalem and forbade Jewish religious practices. The Jews revolted and, through a series of brilliant military campaigns, were able to defeat the Seleucids and so secure a brief period of independence for Judah (about 142-63 B.C.). This period, of the so-called Hasmonaean kingdom, was brought to an end by a bitter civil war which was only stopped when Rome, the power that finally drove the Seleucids from Syria, intervened. In 63 B.C. the Roman general Pompey entered Jerusalem. The area, now called Judaea, was given semi-independence in 40 B.C., when the Roman senate, in recognition of his loyalty to Rome, appointed Herod king. Herod's son Archelaus succeeded his father in 4 B.C., but he was unsatisfactory as a ruler. In A.D. 6 he was dismissed by Augustus, leaving Judaea as a Roman province of the third class, ruled by officials called procurators.

TIME OF CHANGE
Alexander the Great had a vast empire stretching from Greece to western India. The period when Palestine was part of this empire was one of change for the area. Long-standing traditions were overturned in the process of "Hellenism", the full-scale importing of Greek (and later, Roman) culture, including art, architecture, religion, and even language.

WHERE THE ROMAN WRIT RAN
By the time of Titus, the entire Mediterranean area was under Roman rule.

FROM GREECE TO EGYPT
When Alexander died, his empire was fought over by his generals. Ptolemy I, a Macedonian, seized Egypt and Palestine, and founded a dynasty that ruled from a new capital, Alexandria, in Egypt. The Ptolemies were Greek, but were often portrayed as traditional Egyptian rulers. This painted limestone stela shows Ptolemy II, who succeeded his father in 283 B.C.

PORTABLE ALTAR
This miniature bronze altar of the Roman period comes from Byblos. Once an important Phoenician city and port, Byblos became a minor town in the Roman period.

SACRIFICE TO THE GODS
The enforced worship of pagan Greek and Roman gods and goddesses was deeply resented by the Jews.

JEWISH REVOLTS

In A.D. 66 a Jewish revolt against Roman rule, led by high-ranking priests and Pharisees, broke out in Palestine. The revolt was put down with great severity by the emperor Vespasian, together with his son Titus who, in A.D. 70, captured Jerusalem and destroyed the Temple. The last stronghold of the Jews was Masada, which fell to the Romans in A.D. 74 after the mass suicide of the defenders. A second revolt in A.D. 132 was crushed by the emperor Hadrian.

Marble bust of the Roman emperor Tiberius

ARCH OF TITUS

The Roman victory in the first Jewish war was commemorated in sculpted friezes on a magnificent arch in Rome. The arch was erected by the emperor Domitian in memory of his brother Titus.

CALVARY

After A.D. 6 Judaea was a province of the Roman empire, run by procurators. It was under the fifth procurator, Pontius Pilate (A.D. 27-30), that Jesus Christ was crucified.

CRUCIFIXION

This reconstruction shows how Jesus might have been crucified.

This amusing Roman "face" juglet from Jerusalem was made in a mould. It dates to the 2nd century A.D.

NEW GODS FOR OLD

The Greeks and Romans introduced their own gods and goddesses. In Phoenicia, where Canaanite religion had persisted until the coming of Alexander, most of these could be related to the old gods. The "new" goddess Aphrodite, shown here in a bronze statue from Byblos, was identified with the Canaanite and Phoenician fertility goddess Astarte (pp. 24-25).

ROMAN BURIALS

During the Roman period, burial was a two-stage process. After death, the body was wrapped in linen, sprinkled with perfume, and placed on a shelf inside a tomb. After some time, when the flesh had decayed, the relatives would enter the tomb, gather up the bones, and place them in a stone box called an ossuary.

King Herod

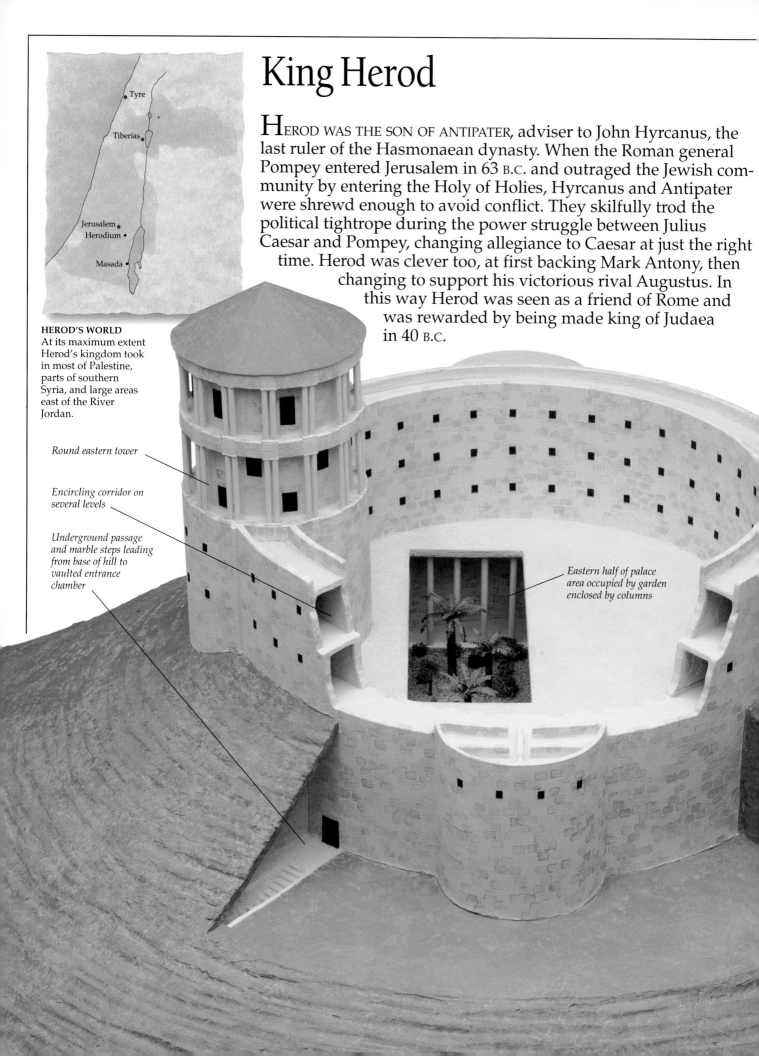

HEROD WAS THE SON OF ANTIPATER, adviser to John Hyrcanus, the last ruler of the Hasmonaean dynasty. When the Roman general Pompey entered Jerusalem in 63 B.C. and outraged the Jewish community by entering the Holy of Holies, Hyrcanus and Antipater were shrewd enough to avoid conflict. They skilfully trod the political tightrope during the power struggle between Julius Caesar and Pompey, changing allegiance to Caesar at just the right time. Herod was clever too, at first backing Mark Antony, then changing to support his victorious rival Augustus. In this way Herod was seen as a friend of Rome and was rewarded by being made king of Judaea in 40 B.C.

HEROD'S WORLD
At its maximum extent Herod's kingdom took in most of Palestine, parts of southern Syria, and large areas east of the River Jordan.

Tyre

Tiberias

Jerusalem
Herodium

Masada

Round eastern tower

Encircling corridor on several levels

Underground passage and marble steps leading from base of hill to vaulted entrance chamber

Eastern half of palace area occupied by garden enclosed by columns

WILD WOMAN
John the Baptist, whose head was brought to Salome, was a prisoner at Herod's fortress at Machaerus. The story is shown in a detail of a painting by Lucas Cranach (1472-1553).

WELL APPOINTED
The western half of the palace area at Herodium contained living quarters and service rooms. On the north side was this impressive bath-house. It was richly ornamented with mosaic floors and frescoes.

HERODIUM *right and below*
Herod was a great builder. Little has survived of his greatest achievement, the rebuilt Temple at Jerusalem. But excavations of his palatial mountain-top fortress around the Jordan Valley and the Dead Sea have shown something of the splendour of his architecture. Herod's hill-top fortress of Herodium, 12 km (8 miles) south of Jerusalem, is a good example. It contained a luxurious palace and was also Herod's burial place. The picture shows an aerial view of the site today; the model is a reconstruction of what it looked like in Herod's time.

WALL OF TEARS
The wailing wall at Jerusalem is part of the western retaining wall of the huge sanctuary that contained Herod's Temple at its centre.

MASSACRE OF THE INNOCENTS
According to the New Testament, it was Herod the Great who was responsible for the slaughter of the children in his attempt to dispose of Jesus of Nazareth. In reality the story is a myth.

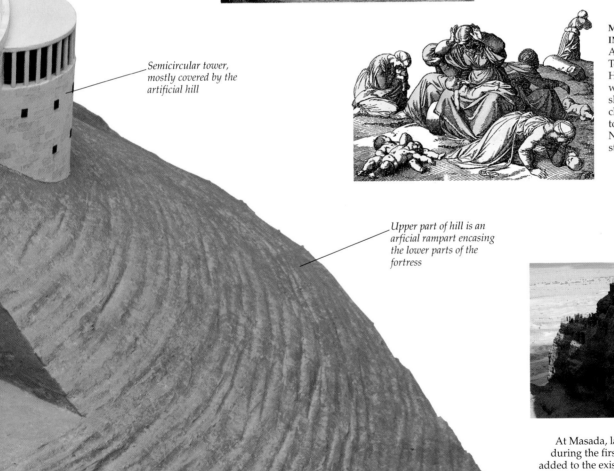

Semicircular tower, mostly covered by the artificial hill

Upper part of hill is an arficial rampart encasing the lower parts of the fortress

MASADA
At Masada, later to become famous during the first Jewish revolt, Herod added to the existing buildings a series of huge water cisterns, store-houses for ammunition and food, and a luxurious palace constructed on three natural rock terraces.

The Bible as evidence

THE BIBLE AS WE KNOW IT today is not a single book, but a collection of 63 individual books, divided into two main parts, the Old and New Testaments. For archaeologists working in the Holy Land, the Bible is a major source, containing a wealth of historical, religious, philosophical, sociological, literary, and poetic material. But it must, like any other ancient collection of texts, be used critically. Many of the Old Testament books are edited compilations, put into their final form a long time after the events they describe. The development of the Bible and the disentangling of the various strands that form its books are fields of study in their own right.

DEAD SEA SCROLLS

In 1947 a goatherd stumbled into a cave at Qumran. It contained the ancient Hebrew manuscripts now called the Dead Sea Scrolls. They had been stored in pottery jars like this one. Although incomplete and fragmentary, the scrolls must originally have included all of the books of the Old Testament and Apocrypha. They are the oldest versions of the texts known so far.

One of the Dead Sea Scrolls contains the text of the Book of Habakkuk, together with a verse-by-verse commentary in which the words of the prophet are set against contemporary events

THE BIBLE IN GREEK

The 4th-century A.D. Codex Sinaiticus is inscribed in Greek capital letters in ink on parchment. It was discovered at the St Catherine's monastery, right.

HIDING PLACE OF THE SCROLLS

Caves in the Judaean Desert, close to the Dead Sea, were the hiding places of the Scrolls. They probably came from the library of Qumran, the monastery of a highly religious group of Jews, the Essenes. The scrolls were put in the caves to protect them from the Romans during the first Jewish revolt (p. 55).

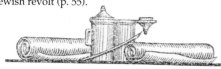

TURIN SHROUD

The Shroud of Turin was long regarded as one of the holiest of Christian relics. It was believed to be the shroud in which Jesus of Nazareth was wrapped following the crucifixion, and bore an extraordinary image said to be that of Christ himself. Modern scientific testing, using radiocarbon analysis, has since shown that it is in fact a medieval fake.

Jesus asking for the children to be brought to him

MOSAIC MAP
In 1884, a remarkable mosaic was discovered in the Greek Orthodox church in Madaba, Jordan. Dating to the 6th century A.D., it depicts a map of the Holy Land with pictures of towns, individual buildings, and other details. Although parts of the map have suffered considerable damage, it preserves a fine illustration of Jerusalem and parts of the Jordan Valley and the Negev.

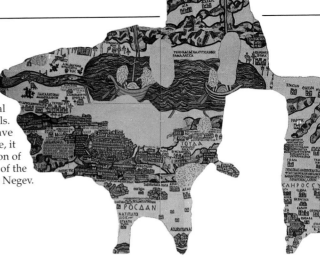

GOSPEL
This page of St Luke's Gospel is from a 5th-century text, the Codex Alexandrinus.

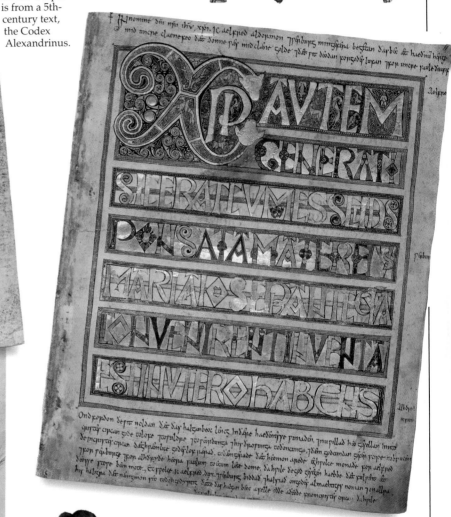

ILLUMINATED MANUSCRIPT
In the Medieval period, highly decorated, or "illuminated", manuscripts of the Bible were produced by monks. This example is from a Latin Bible of around 750, preserved in the Royal Library in Stockholm.

BEFORE THE CRUCIFIXION
This portrayal of Christ wearing the crown of thorns is by the 15th-century Flemish painter Quentin Massys.

Continued on next page

Continued from previous page

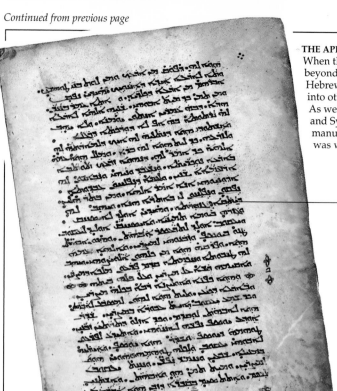

— *Text in Syriac*

THE APPEARANCE OF TRANSLATIONS
When the Christian church spread beyond the areas where Greek and Hebrew were spoken, translations into other languages began to appear. As well as Bibles in Latin, Egyptian and Syriac Bibles appeared. This manuscript of the New Testament was written in 1216 in Syriac.

MOSES AND THE TABLETS
When Moses returned from Mount Sinai he brought with him stone tablets engraved with the law.

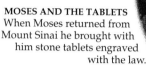

Text in Hebrew —

SCROLLS OF THE SYNAGOGUE
Hebrew scribes meticulously copied out the texts of the Old Testament books on to parchment. These were rolled up and kept in the Jewish places of worship, the synagogues.

HEBREW BIBLE
This page from a Hebrew Bible shows the story of the Exodus. This is quite a recent Hebrew Bible, but the text has changed very little since the Dead Sea Scrolls were written out almost 2,000 years ago.

Scrolls covered in fine cloth

JESUS IN THE TEMPLE
The young Jesus was once discovered in discussion with the wise men at the Temple. This story shows the importance of scholarship and debate for the Jews – a tradition which has continued to this day. The episode is shown here in a painting by William Holman Hunt.

THE MENORAH
The Hebrew word "menorah" means a lampstand. In the Old Testament it refers specifically to the seven-branched candlestick which stood in the Temple of Jerusalem and later became a Jewish symbol. The menorah was removed from the Temple by the Romans in A.D. 70. It is depicted, with other objects similarly looted, in the carvings on the arch of Titus.

THE FIRST PRINTED BIBLE
Johannes Gutenberg was one of the inventors of printing with movable type in the 15th century. His Bible, which appeared in 1456, was the first printed edition. The text was in Latin. Printed texts made the Bible much more accessible. Soon, printed translations of the Bible into the modern European languages started to roll off the press.

KING DAVID
David was the second king of Israel. According to the Bible he began his career as a shepherd boy and was the writer of the Psalms. He is shown here in a painting by Pietro Perugino (1446-1523).

Text in Latin

Text in English

THE BIBLE IN ENGLISH
English translations of the Bible began to appear with Wycliffe's version in 1384. William Tyndale was the first English translator to tackle the New Testament. His New Testament first appeared in 1526. It had to be smuggled into England because there was so much opposition to translations of the original biblical texts.

An Arab encampment painted by David Roberts (1796-1864)

Archaeology

W. M. F. PETRIE
Petrie had already made a considerable reputation for himself in Egypt when he was appointed by the Palestine Exploration Fund.

MODERN ARCHAEOLOGY in the Holy Land began in 1865 with the formation of the Palestine Exploration Fund. The purpose of the fund was to investigate the archaeology, geography, geology, and natural history of Palestine. A detailed survey was completed in 1877, and with accurate maps to hand, archaeology could begin. In 1890 the Fund engaged Flinders Petrie to excavate at Tell el-Hesi. The results were highly influential. Petrie knew exactly what a tell was (pp. 14-15), and developed a system to reveal the complicated series of occupation layers one by one. Petrie had established the principles of "stratigraphic" archaeology, still used today.

HAND PICK
A small hand pick is ideally suited to the soil conditions in the Holy Land, breaking up the earth cleanly and causing minimal damage to any underlying features or artefacts.

Metal bob hangs vertically

SURVEYOR'S POLE
A ranging pole, 2 m (6 ft) long and marked off in red and white 50-cm (20-in) bands is used not only in surveying but also as a convenient indicator of scale in excavation photographs.

KEEPING VERTICALS VERTICAL
A plumb-line is used in planning and making vertical sections. A section through a site is the archaeologists's most valuable resource, providing a visual record of the site's sequence of occupation layers.

BETH SHAN
Petrie understood that a tell, like Beth Shan, had formed over generations by the build-up of debris. Archaeologists remove the layers one-by-one, in reverse chronological order. The objects found within each layer are specific to that layer, so studying them shows how the culture of the people changed over the centuries.

GENTLE LEVER *right*
A plasterer's "leaf" is a sensitive tool used for isolating fragile objects from the soil and lifting them up.

GENERAL SIR CHARLES WARREN
Warren investigated Jerusalem on behalf of the Palestine Exploration Fund. The work was very dangerous, involving the sinking of deep shafts, but it provided much information about the construction of the Dome of the Rock and the platform of Herod's Temple.

10m 2kg B.S.4484

TAKING MEASUREMENTS
Precision is essential in archaeology. Cloth tapes are used, in conjunction with surveying instruments such as theodolites, to set out the excavation areas and to make accurate plans of excavated features.

TROWELS
The standard tool of the archaeologist is the trowel. In the Holy Land trowels are not used so much for digging, where their scraping action can cause considerable damage. They are used for cleaning away the soil after it has been broken up with a hand-pick and for cutting vertical "section" faces through the soil.

SIR CHARLES WILSON
The establishment of the Palestine Exploration Fund was partly inspired by a highly successful survey of Jerusalem undertaken in 1864 by Wilson and a team of Royal Engineers.

SINAI SURVEYORS
In 1868-1869 the Palestine Exploration Fund mounted an expedition to southern Sinai in order to examine the possible routes of the Exodus. The survey work was carried out by Captain Wilson (shown at the rear smoking a pipe).

HOLD-ALL
For work in the field some sort of site bag is essential for carrying equipment – notebooks, pens, tapes, nails, string, spirit levels, labels, bags for finds, and countless other items.

Strap fits around waist

HANDY RULE
Small 2-m (6-ft) or 3-m (9-ft) steel tapes are invaluable for planning, section drawing, and measuring excavated features and objects.

Index

Acknowledgments

Dorling Kindersley would like to thank:
Jacquie Gulliver for help with the initial stages of producing the book; Céline Carez, Bernadette Crowley, and Claire Gillard for editorial assistance; Jane Parker for the index; Lisa Bliss, Kevin Lovelock, and John Williams of the British Museum for additional photography; Liz Sephton for design assistance; and Peter Akkermans, Rupert L. Chapman, Samantha Bolden, Peter Dorrell, Peter Rea, Dianne Rowan, and Kathryn W. Tubb for further assistance.

Maps Eugene Fleury
Models David Donkin

Picture credits

t=top, b=bottom, c=centre, l=left, r=right

J. C. Allen: 7b, 23cb, 59tr.
Ancient Art & Architecture Collection: 43tl, 61tl.
Ashmolean Museum, Oxford: 38c.
Birmingham Museum and Art Galleries: 60b.
Werner Braun: 6b, 27tl, 57cr.
Bridgeman Art Library: 50br detail, 57tr detail; /Atkinson Art Gallery, Southport 61b; /Bible Society, London 58cr, 59cl, 60tl, 61cr; /Christies, London 38bl, 61cl; /Gavin Graham Gallery, London 32cl detail; /Guildhall Library 12b, 42c detail; /Musée des Beaux-Arts, Nantes 61tr; /Prado, Madrid 59br; /Private Collection 28tr, 60cl; /Royal Library Stockholm, 59cr; /Victoria & Albert Museum, London 30tr detail.

Trustees of the British Museum, London: 8bl, 15tr, 18bl, 19b, 42cr.
Dr. P. Dorrell, Institute of Archaeology: 8cr.
Egyptian Museum, Cairo: 20c.
E. T. Archive, Victoria & Albert Museum: 7tl.
Mary Evans Picture Library: 21br, 26tl, 41cr, 44tr.
Giraudon Louvre: 41tl.
Sonia Halliday Photographs: 6tl, 6cl, 14bl, 43c, 55tc, 62c.
Hamburger Kunsthalle: 34br detail, 46tl detail.
Robert Harding Picture Library: 10cl, 49br, 52bl, 58cl.
Michael Holford: 22-23b, 28tl, 35cl, 38, 41cl, 46-47.
Dept. of Antiquities, Israel Museum: front jacket cl, 17t, 24bl, 35bc, 43tr, 58cl.
Kobal Collection: 37c.
Kunsthistorisches Museum, Vienna: 10-11b.

Mansell Collection: 59tl.
National Gallery, London: 30br detail, 55cl detail.
National Maritime Museum, Haifa: 4041b.
Palestine Exploration Fund: 62tl, 62bl, 63tl, 63br.
Zev Radovan: 6cb, 13cl, 15tl, 15cl, 17cr, 27tr, 57c.
Scala: 55tl.
Jamie Simpson: 12c.
Sotheby's, London: 7tr.
Amoret Tanner: front jacket tl, back jacket bl, 12tl, 28cb, 29tl, 29bc, 32tr, 33br.
Victoria & Albert Museum: 59bl.
Zefa; 7c, 50bl.